We

e, and

e

Paperback ISBN: 978-
eBook ISBN: 978-1-9

Contents

Acknowledgments

This book would not have happened without the encouragement of a few women near and dear to me. My life coach, spiritual advisor, and best friend all told me they thought I could help people with grief someday. Years later, a new friend, who is a grief counselor, thought I could help too, and she suggested I write down my story, the whole thing. This book is an unexpected enrichment to my life thanks to their friendship and encouragement.

Chapter One

Introduction

I have been a photo hobbyist my entire adult life. One of my favorite photo projects is a slideshow about my life. My inspiration came from slideshows that are created by loved ones when someone dies. I wondered how different a slideshow that I created for me would be from one created by a loved one after I was gone. That's how it started. However, it ended up as a photo journal reflecting my immense gratitude for all the amazing ways I've been lucky enough to enjoy this life and this spectacular planet! I call it my Gratitude Album.

The project wasn't about all my wonderful family, friends, or places I've traveled to. That's because I have thousands of photos of people and places, and I would be overwhelmed! I kept it simple. I included my husband, mom, dad, stepmom, and favorite aunt. I included my cat, dogs, and horses. Who would think of including my fur babies in the slideshow besides me? The rest of the pictures represent me living my life outside - having a blast! The pictures include sports, hobbies, and active adventures such as kayaking, skydiving, mountain biking, scuba diving, and much more. The album is special to me, and I love it! I encourage everyone to create their own gratitude album!

This book starts with a story about my gratitude album slideshow because when I share my slideshow with others, they think about various things, such as their special memory of a place I'm pictured in and how they relate to it. Something in any picture can create a connection and spark thoughts. I think that's natural and great! That's my hope for this book. I'm sharing my story as a one-sided conversation, and I hope others will relate to it in a meaningful way. If something I share inspires or helps someone, that's even better!

We are all one.
We are all human.
We laugh, We cry, We love, and We die.

We dream and create. We help others and are helped by others. We give, and we get. Our lives are created and re-created by the choices we make all day, every day. What a remarkable journey life is!

Chapter Two

Birth through High School

1961 to 1979

My life journey began in November 1961 in Albuquerque, NM, with my mom, dad, and older sister. By the age of two, my mom and dad divorced. My dad married my stepmom, and they had a daughter and a son together. My mom married my stepdad, who had two daughters, and they had a son together. My older sister and I stayed with Mom. My family of seven included my mom, stepdad, older sister, two older stepsisters, and one younger half-brother. My dad's family of four included my dad, stepmom, younger half-sister, and younger half-brother.

My parents remained good friends, and both families got along well. We all enjoyed spending time together. My older sister and I vacationed with Dad's family to visit his parents in Texas and my stepmom's parents in Colorado. My family of seven went on camping trips and road trips over the years. I thought I was lucky to have two families!

My mom is fully Danish, which makes me half-Danish. This is an interesting story about my Danish heritage. Mom's maternal grandmother came to America from Denmark through Ellis Island in New York City in 1903 at the age of eighteen with her younger sister, who was sixteen. They were detained at Ellis Island because of their age for three months until arrangements could be made for their friends in America to come and get them. Her boyfriend did not want to go to America at first. He decided he couldn't live without her, so he followed her here and married her. They had two children - my grandmother and her brother. My grandmother married a Danish man, and they had two children - my mom and her brother. Later in my life, I was in New York for work, and I visited Ellis Island. I was shown the ledger where my great-grandmother and her sister signed in, and I saw the building where they were detained. That was a powerful experience, and I wasn't expecting to get as emotional as I did. What a brave thing they did at such a young age!

When I was nine, we moved from Albuquerque to the village of Corrales, which is across the Rio Grande River to the northwest. We lived in a beautiful, old adobe house that was built in the 1840s. The house was built by a Spaniard sent from Spain to settle the territory when the area belonged to Spain. The area became part of Mexico and then the USA within a ten-year period. I loved growing up in Corrales, and especially in that house. We all did! The village is a beautiful, unique, and historic community that borders the Rio Grande River. The main road was the only paved road. There are many old adobe churches, and tall, sculptural cottonwood trees dominate the landscape. The majestic Sandia Mountains to the east of Albuquerque create a great backdrop. Sandia means watermelon, and at sunset, the mountains turn a wonderful watermelon-pink color. What a special gift for everyone who lives there!

The house was furnished with beautiful rugs, paintings, and pottery from Native American artists, as well as solid, hand-carved furniture from Mexico. Mom owned a store where she sold this beautiful art and furniture. We were invited and privileged to visit the Native American communities and enjoy their beautiful dances. I'll never forget seeing the Snake Dance. The dancers danced with live snakes! Snakes were slithering around on the ground and were carried! I watched from behind my stepdad, just in case. A passion for the art of the Southwest was instilled in me for life. I'll take silver and turquoise over gold and diamonds every time!

One summer, when I was young, my family drove to Mexico City, Mexico in mom's large delivery truck from her store. We toured the incredible three-story factory where the Mexican furniture was made that Mom sold in her store. The factory was open to the public and included a restaurant, a store and much more. There were different rooms where visitors could watch artisans through a large window blowing glass fixtures or hand carving furniture. We spent an entire day there and it was impressive! Mom introduced us to some high-level Mexican dignitaries she knew, and they told us they valued and appreciated my mom and her commerce. That made an unforgettable impression on me, and I felt proud and happy for my mom! I may have clapped a little bit. We all enjoyed shopping at the various street markets. I'll always remember the vibrant paintings on black velvet, and the colorful wood marionettes that were intricately hand-carved, and beautifully decorated. I loved Mexico City! I grew up around the Hispanic culture in Corrales. I learned Spanish, and I love mariachi music and Mexican food. I'll put green chili on almost anything!

My siblings and I were animal lovers. I had a wonderful horse that I rode everywhere, oftentimes barefoot and bareback. Riding my horse was for enjoyment and as transportation to my babysitting jobs. Sometimes, I rode home from babysitting in the dark under the moon and stars, which was lovely. Over the years, we had dogs, cats, horses, rabbits, and chickens. I had a pet sheep and a large white turkey that liked to sit (and poop) on the back of my horse, and a pair of peacocks came with the house.

The house was added to over the years and included a back apartment, penthouse, swimming pool, and beautiful courtyards. The center of the house is called the Sala (ballroom). The Sala is large and a great place for entertaining and dancing, and we hosted many large parties for people from around the world. The next image is a drawing of the entrance to the Sala by my artistic mom.

The house was historic and haunted! Living in a haunted house is a unique experience. We had many mysterious and unexplained things happen (hauntings). The hauntings started right after we moved in and were basically harmless. For example, items were moved around or would disappear and then magically reappeared later. When Mom's very special Hopi watch disappeared, we looked everywhere for it; I mean everywhere! Two years later, right before we moved out, Mom found the Hopi watch lying out on a shelf in her closet! She was excited and thought I'd found it and placed it there. I did not, and there was no one else in the house. How did it get there!? Previous occupants of the house had many stories about hauntings, and they wrote about them. One recurring story has to do with orange peels showing up in the strangest places. We found one up high in a candle chandelier that hung over the dining room table. Hmmm, why orange peels? Once, I was sweeping the living room brick floor when the room temperature suddenly turned ice cold. The hair on my neck stood up, and I got goosebumps. I stopped sweeping, and I froze. It was eerie. The cats and dogs who were in the room with me as I cleaned suddenly jumped up and left together in a hurry. I put down the broom and followed them!

Many incredible, fascinating, mysterious, and unbelievable things happened during my time in the house. I was not afraid to live there because I knew we were safe. Living in a haunted house was an extraordinary experience that shaped my life in unique ways. I believe in reincarnation and that our souls make many journeys to live temporarily in the physical realm, and then our souls return home to the other side when we die. For me, the only explanation for the mysterious hauntings is magic from the other side. Everything in the universe is made from energy, including matter and us. I believe magic is the manipulation of energy and matter to create mysteries and miracles that cannot be explained by science. I could be right about this. Who's to say for sure?

After ten years of marriage, my mom and stepdad divorced. My two older stepsisters and younger brother moved to Denver with their dad. The divorce was hard, but we all remained a family and continued to visit and spend time together whenever possible throughout our lives. My older sister got married young and had my niece by this time. In my high school years, it was down to just me and my mom in the house. Mom and I were ideal roommates. She was a wonderful cook and did most of the cooking. We shared the responsibilities of cleaning, shopping, and taking care of the animals. The only television in the house was in her bedroom, and we enjoyed hanging out together on her king-size waterbed watching TV.

My older sisters' family and their friends were around the house a lot. I loved spending time with my adorable little niece. Isn't the laughter of a small child the greatest sound!? Some of their friends were musicians, and they would entertain us for hours in the living room, singing and playing guitars. That was so fun and very special! My brother-in-law was a big guy with a surprisingly sweet singing voice, and I loved listening to him sing. He could hit some high notes! One of their friends lived in the back apartment, and he played his guitar and sang for me on the patio. Nice! I have no musical talent, and I greatly admire talented musicians. This was the only time in my life I was around music in this way, and I cherish the memories! The iconic song - 'House of the Rising Sun' always takes me back to this time.

My high school years were great! I had many good friends, my mom included, and we navigated life together. My life was filled with the ups and downs typical of that time of life. One of my best friends was five years older than me, and we rode our horses together regularly. My mom, stepmom, and favorite aunt were smart, successful, professional women. Mom was a graduate of a prestigious university and a successful entrepreneur, my stepmom was a medical doctor, and my aunt has a doctorate in nutrition. Looking back, my stepsister and I never doubted that we could be successful at whatever we chose to do because of them. We're grateful for having strong, smart, independent women as role models in our lives. *Fun Fact:* My pretty mom was recruited to be a model for Neiman Marcus one summer when she was in college.

In the 1970s women earned sixty cents compared to a dollar for the same job as a man. The gap has gotten smaller, but it's still not equal pay in the 2020s! The wheels of equality for women turn very slowly in a man's world. Through my experience and observations, I learned that women must work harder than men for equal recognition, which isn't fair or right. Fortunately, women have made huge strides toward equality, and today's generation has it better than my mom's generation did.

During my last semester in high school, one of my best friends and I went on a road trip to tour colleges in Colorado and find the best one for me. I love Colorado, and I was happy when my mom and dad agreed to let me move there to attend college. We had a great adventure in my friend's orange Ford pickup truck with the manual gear shift in the steering column. We attempted to lose the only set of truck keys, but someone found them and put them on the truck antenna. I attempted to lose my wallet with all my cash, but someone found it and returned it with the cash in it. Luck was with us, and disasters were avoided! We drove over mountain passes through snowbanks as tall as the truck on our way to Durango, which was our last stop. I stood on top of the mesa where the campus is, taking in the view of the beautiful Animas valley and river below and the majestic La Plata Mountains to the west. I knew right then that Durango couldn't be beat. *Fun Fact:* My friend is a Sioux Indian, and she became a lawyer focused on defending the rights of Native Americans.

Chapter Three

The College Years

1979 – 1984

In 1979, at age seventeen, I graduated from high school and moved to Durango to go to college. I had to sell my horse, which was very hard. The father of the girl I sold her to gave me a kind hug and said he could see my tears behind my sunglasses. Mom sold the house in Corrales and moved to Albuquerque. We both returned to visit the house in Corrales over the years, just like previous occupants did when we lived there. The house has a special quality that stays in your heart forever. Owners came and went, and it was never loved like it was when we lived there. Sadly, our once proud home became neglected and run down, and I stopped visiting because it was too sad to watch. After many years, a new owner fell in love with it. He repaired and modernized the old house while keeping its historic qualities, and he had the house registered as a historic site. I had the pleasure of meeting him, and we toured the house. It filled my heart with joy to see this beautiful, old house come back to life! He eventually sold the house and moved to California. The new owner fell in love with the house, too! Interestingly, I've visited her and her staff, and they all feel a strong connection to the house. It's now a place to shop and a place to get married! I'm so happy for all the people who get to enjoy it. The stories of hauntings have stopped, which I think is part of the changes that time brings.

The choice to go to college in Durango was excellent! What a beautiful place! The skiing was great, and I had many good friends and many fun things to do. I especially loved working for a rafting company one summer and enjoying great river adventures. My stand-out river adventure happened when we rafted through Cataract Canyon in Canyonlands, Utah. There was a rapid called Big Drop, which was a huge spillover waterfall that fell into a large raft-eating hole. There were five rafts on the trip, and my friend and I were on the last raft to go through Big Drop. We watched all the other rafts get flipped over in the hole. We couldn't see the hole, but we saw the upside-down rafts as they appeared further downriver. My friend is one of the most skilled oarswomen I know, and I was thankful to be in her raft. We were nervous, and she stood as we approached the drop-off, looking for the best line. My heart was pounding! I was crouched down in the front of the raft with a death grip on the ropes. She nailed it! We came through it still upright! What a thrill! When we eddied out in calm water with the other rafts, we jumped up and hugged each other. In my excitement, I fell off the raft backward into the river and had to be pulled back onto the raft. That was embarrassing! Nevertheless, it was funny, and we all laughed.

In the spring of 1982, I had the opportunity of a lifetime to go to New Zealand for a five-week college geology course. There were twenty-two of us, including our guide and professor. One friend and I were the only two girls! New Zealand is a stunningly beautiful country encompassing two islands. The geology has everything from ocean beaches and rainforests to glaciers and volcanoes. I fell in love with the magnificent landscape and the people who live there, with their kind ways and simple lifestyle. As America was heading into summer, New Zealand was heading into winter. My stand-out adventure was backpacking on the world-renowned Milford Sound Trek. The hike took three days. We were rained on a lot and were pretty wet the whole time. It even snowed on us on the highest pass on the trail! That was unfortunate because we missed an epic view. We slept in huts with wood stoves. We hung our wet clothes on clotheslines inside the huts, but it was never enough to dry everything out. The upside to all the rain was all the beautiful waterfalls! We would've preferred nice weather, but I wouldn't trade that experience for anything. However, I hope I never have to smell wet wool socks ever again! We packed in a lot of sightseeing and schooling, and the five weeks went by way too fast. New Zealand was a grand adventure, and I got an A for the course!

In 1983, at age twenty-one, I graduated from college with a self-constructed major in Business/Energy Science. I had to present my major for approval to the college President and the Board of Directors. The process was an interesting and challenging experience. I had similar majors from other colleges to use as examples. My major was approved as a Bachelor of Arts degree. Originally, I chose Accounting/Finance as my major. Then, I took environmental science classes that had a huge impact on me, so I switched majors in my junior year.

I was going to help save the world by guiding businesses and people to make smart choices about energy use. I felt it was important to turn the tables on the damage being done to the planet from our thirst for energy, especially oil and gas. Carbon pollution is just one of many global environmental issues that need to be addressed. Unfortunately, my fellow advocates and I were way ahead of our time. The solutions were going to take money and sacrifice, and the world wasn't ready for that. Theodore Roosevelt (twenty-sixth USA president) said it best; "Burning fossil fuels is like breaking up the furniture to feed the fireplace because it's easier than going out to the woodpile."

We knew that a worldwide population that grew exponentially was a serious concern. When I brought it up, I was told no one has the right to tell anyone how many children they can have. I agree. Unfortunately, it seems that people prefer to avoid the topic of overpopulation. The world population was under five billion back then, and it's at eight billion now. Where will our world population be in ten years? Water is another serious concern. When are we going to stop wasting it? I don't mean to lecture, but this is what I have studied, and I can't help myself! It's taken literal decades since then for the world to take action to solve the many global problems. We must try! This planet is our shared home. Fortunately, there are always smart people worldwide doing incredible things that matter and make a difference.

There was a new political party in charge in the white house, and the programs and job opportunities where I could use my degree disappeared overnight, mostly through funding cuts and eliminating energy tax credits. After college, I made one attempt to use my college degree by selling energy control devices in Colorado Springs. I enjoyed the consulting part but not the selling part, and I decided it wasn't the right fit. I had to do something to pay the bills, so I went back to plan A with the accounting career.

In 1984, one year after graduating from college, I moved from Colorado Springs back to Corrales, into my older high school best friend's home. My first job was with my older sister at a business that repaired hot air balloons. That was a fun job! Mom taught me how to sew when I was seven. Who knew that skill would land me a cool job later in life? I enjoyed many exciting adventures in hot air ballooning, the best one being the year I flew in the Albuquerque International Balloon Fiesta mass ascension. It was spectacular! If you ever get a chance to see the event, you must go! Hundreds of balloons fill the sky, and there's nothing else like it in the world. The fascinating thing about ballooning is that the wind is moving the balloon, so inside the gondola basket it's perfectly quiet and calm. I've had some great landings and some not-so-great landings. As we were touching down after the mass ascension, a wind gust knocked the basket over, and the two large men in it landed on top of me and knocked the wind out of me! They scrambled out of the basket, and I caught my breath. Whew!

I felt like a dog with my tail between my legs because this was not the plan I'd made in college. I especially didn't see myself leaving Colorado and moving back home! However, the universe had me right on course. I met my husband almost immediately. My friend (and roommate) was his friend, and she introduced us to each other at a bar. My friend and I joined him and his roommate for beers and socializing a few times. In July, we all went to a rodeo in Santa Fe. By the end of that day, it was clear who had the best chemistry in the group, and he asked me out on a dinner date. We were headed to town for dinner when he pulled off the road. He leaned over and kissed me and then got back on the road. He said he wanted to get that out of the way. That worked for me! At dinner, we found ourselves holding hands across the table for quite a while. Who does that on the first date? We were so lost in our own world that we hadn't noticed the restaurant was empty, and the staff was putting chairs on the tables until the waiter politely asked if we would please leave so they could close. We laughed at ourselves as we walked to the car, holding hands.

In August, he invited me to join him in Crested Butte, CO for his best friend's wedding. He was the best man. I remember watching this tall, handsome cowboy making his toast to the couple, and I just couldn't take my eyes off him. We had such a good time, and we started falling in love. We dated for four months, then we lived together for four months, then we were engaged for four months, then we got married the following August.

When we met, I was twenty-two, and he was twenty-six. I loved the single life. I never thought about marriage, and I didn't see the point to it anyway since I wasn't planning to have children. My husband felt the same way. After living together for a few months, it became clear that we wanted to spend the rest of our lives together, and marriage was on our minds. One Sunday evening, after watching a football game, we were having a beer, and my husband said he'd been thinking a lot about buying a house and that he was ready to take that step. I agreed that paying for a mortgage was smarter than paying for someone else's mortgage through rent. I asked how I fit into this scenario. He said he would not want to buy a house together unless we were married. He asked me how I felt about that. He was staring deep into my eyes, searching them, and I was doing the same. Finally, I smiled and said I would love to be his wife. We started kissing a lot! When we came up for air, I said Hey, shouldn't you be on one knee or something? He said Hey, shouldn't you be crying or something? We laughed and kissed some more. The next day he came home after work with the perfect engagement and wedding ring set. Since it wasn't entirely clear who proposed to whom, he liked to tell people that I proposed to him, and I would just smile. I tell people we accidentally got engaged one day. It was perfect for us, and I wouldn't change a thing.

Chapter Four

Married Life in New Mexico

1985 to 1999

In August 1985, at age twenty-three, I married the love of my life, my soul mate, my very best friend, and the half that makes me whole. We love each other as deeply as two people possibly can. Those of you who know, know. I'd had other relations with men but never fell in love. It was all a little scary at first to fall that deeply in love with someone and to have someone fall that deeply in love with me. Meeting him was the best thing that ever happened to me!

We held our wedding in the Sandia Mountains. Most of my relatives of all generations from both families were there to share our special day, along with many of my husband's relatives and our closest friends, including two of my best friends from high school. It's a very special and joyous event to have so many people you care about all together, having a good time, and enjoying each other. There were dark clouds threatening to rain on us. When it was time for the ceremony to start, the clouds parted, and the sun shone down brightly on us! I'm pretty sure I heard angels singing. Our wedding day was the happiest day of my life!

We became a great team. We faced the world together. We were stronger together. We were very compatible, and our lives were enriched by our shared interests. We enjoyed the same music, movies, books, hobbies, and sports, with a few exceptions. We did almost everything together. When I did things without him, I wished he was there. We lived an active lifestyle that kept us outside most of the time. My husband called us outdoor dogs. We worked hard and played hard, and we loved to dance with each other. One of my favorite memories happened at a corporate Christmas party when we were dancing to a waltz. My husband looked dashing, and I wore a flowing dress. We were lost in the music, the dance, and each other as we covered the dance floor from end-to-end twirling about. We hadn't noticed when the dance floor became empty except for us. People were circled around watching us dance. When the music ended and we stopped, they clapped for us. Wow!

For the next thirty-plus years, we built a great life together. We also endured some very hard times, which is all part of being human.

In the very beginning, we cut our honeymoon short by a day because my husband was having night sweats. He was diagnosed with stage-two Hodgkin's Disease cancer! This was hard news for newlyweds! I cried silently in his hospital room while he slept. He was treated with radiation. I was helpless to help him. The best I could do was stroke his back in the middle of the night when he was getting sick. I drove him to treatments, too. Months later, the cancer went into remission. The treatments ended, and the burned skin on his neck could finally heal. He was so tough through it all! The whole process was hard, but he never once complained. He scheduled his treatments for Fridays. He would be sick on the weekend, so he could go back to work on Monday. He couldn't always make it back on Monday. Even though it was a temporary situation, his boss fired him, and we lost his health insurance. I'll never understand how people can be so cruel and kick someone when they're down.

Fortunately, he found work easily after the treatments ended, and the new job was at a better company. Unfortunately, we could not get affordable insurance for him for years because of his "preexisting condition." Insurance was available for the outrageous cost of $10,000 for six months! We were finally able to get insurance again when a New Mexico state-funded insurance program was created for those who were unable to get affordable insurance due to "preexisting conditions."

Sadly, people act differently around someone with cancer. My husband turned thirty during his battle with cancer. I threw a birthday party for him at a favorite bar. I invited a dozen people. Only two came. He didn't care about that. He had a cynical nature and didn't hold high expectations of people. I'm sure that the others had their reasons for not coming, and that's okay. However, I was disappointed, and my feelings were hurt. We had a great time with the couple that did show up. We danced, and celebrated, and ate birthday cake! We learned a very important life lesson. We, mostly me, made a promise.

Anytime someone is nice enough to invite us to something, then we would be nice enough to say yes and to show up!

Sometimes, an invitation was something we weren't excited about, but we said yes and went anyway. We figured we could always leave after half an hour. We ended up meeting interesting and fun people that we would not have met otherwise, and we always enjoyed ourselves. Sometimes, that deal to leave after half an hour would turn into some of the last to leave instead. A good promise to live by and one filled with rewards.

We became homeowners soon after marriage. We parked our new doublewide mobile home on a two-acre lot we purchased in a rural area south of Albuquerque. My husband was a self-proclaimed desert rat, and he loved the vastness of the arid landscape. He was a bull rider for years. He'd quit riding bulls just before we met because he broke one too many bones. I'm glad he'd quit. I wouldn't have enjoyed watching him ride bulls - too stressful!

He came into the marriage with a pretty Mustang horse that he broke and trained and a macho terrier dog that blew into his yard with the tumbleweeds. I was excited to have a horse to ride again! I came into the marriage with a smart, beautiful, amazing dog and my precious Siamese cat. I'd had them both since high school. The small terrier thought he was every bit as tough as my large dog, and they were a fun, odd pair. Our family grew with the addition of a sweet yellow labrador. My husband was a bird hunter, and she was supposed to be his bird retriever. She hated guns and wanted nothing to do with birds. Go figure. Once, we watched her walk through a group of quail birds in the yard. They split and went around her, and she ignored them. My husband sighed; she was hopeless. I thought it was funny! She was perfect otherwise.

Mom was married to her third husband, and they were very happy together. They threw many fun parties for everyone to get together. We all got along great and shared many good times together, and their bar-b-ques were the best! My mom and stepmom liked each other a lot. When we were all together, they'd be deep in conversation, and Dad told me he'd feel forgotten and wonder, how did this happen?

In 1989, after three years of remission and good health, the Hodgkin's cancer came back at stage four! Hodgkin's is one of only three curable cancers, which gave us hope. This time, the treatment was chemotherapy for eight months. Again, he scheduled his treatments for Fridays to continue working. Again, I was helpless to help him, and I drove him to his treatments. Again, he did what he had to do and never complained. The toughest person I know. I was tough, too, because I believed in him and in us. We supported each other. The chemo treatments were done in a room with other patients, each in their own recliner. He shared with me his observations during that time; those who were bitter or gave up got worse, and those who had hope got better. He had hope, and he got better. Then came the great news - he was cured! Not in remission - cured! What a fantastic, happy thing to hear and to share with all our loved ones. Yay! Let's celebrate!

Thoughts are energy, and they matter!
Pay attention to your thoughts, day and night.
Think about what you think about and how it makes you feel.
Believe in the power of positive thinking!
Choose hope!

Eight months is a very long time when your life is in limbo, and everything is that much harder. We got sideways with each other halfway through the treatments. We were short with each other, and occasionally argued. It was a terrible feeling. One day, we took a ride on the Sandia Peak Tram to get out and enjoy ourselves. Halfway up the mountain I had a panic attack! My palms were sweating, yet I was freezing. My heart was pounding, and my hands were shaking. I felt disoriented and panicked! I didn't know what was happening to me. Was I suddenly claustrophobic, or afraid of heights? We stayed at the top of the mountain until the panic attack passed, and I calmed down. Then I had to get back in the Tram to go home! I sat with my head in my hands and my eyes closed, while my husband rubbed my back to keep me calm. If you've ever had a panic attack, you know how scary that is! One night we snapped at each other over nothing, and I left the living room and went into the sunroom. I thought about it, and then I said to him, we're not mad at each other, we're mad at the damn cancer! We learned a very important life lesson.

When life feels out of control, we take out our stress on the people we feel the safest with.
We learned to never take each other for granted.

For the rest of our lives, we never, ever took each other, or anything we had, for granted. I'm so grateful for learning that very important lesson early in life.

Sadly, my precious cat died a year after we were married. She was very loved and had a good long life. My husband's macho terrier died after that, and within five years, my beautiful, amazing dog died after a good long life. I cried so much! He was my best friend for so long, through it all, since high school. I have a memory from college of sitting in the backyard on the concrete steps, having a little cry, though I don't remember why I was upset. My beautiful, amazing dog came and sat next to me and leaned on me. I put my arm around him and my head on his. He was comforting me, and I felt better. Thanks buddy, I needed that. We soon added a gorgeous red Siberian husky with blue eyes to the family. Our sweet labrador loved my first dog very much. She did not take well to the new one. All the husky wanted to do was play. All the lab wanted was for him to leave her alone. They compromised by her laying pinned to the ground while he jumped back and forth over her. Whatever works! Eventually, they became buddies.

After six years we wanted someplace better to live so we sold our land and moved our doublewide to a two-acre lot we purchased in the town of Edgewood located on the east side of the Sandia Mountains. Just before we moved, my husband sold his pretty Mustang horse, which was a difficult choice but the right choice. She was in her prime and needed regular exercise that we couldn't provide. We sold her to a coworker of mine who was very excited, and we felt like we did the right thing for her. It was heart-breaking when we watched her driving away in the horse trailer and she looked back and whinnied to my husband. Our new land was a nice improvement. We built a huge deck to enjoy our beautiful views. We could see all the way to the mountains around Santa Fe, fifty miles away!

Right after we moved to Edgewood in 1991, my husband's father succumbed to cancer. It was fast between diagnosis and death. He was a war veteran. His ashes were scattered on our property with loved ones around. My husband honored his dad's wish and scattered his ashes on a large prickly cactus. His mom needed us now. She had my husband late in life and was up in years. There's not much I want to say about his father; however, his mom was a sweetheart. His older brother died tragically before I met him. I would've liked to have known his brother.

His mom was able to live independently for years, and we enjoyed her very much. My husband took her shopping, and we took good care of her. She was losing her vision which made her talk louder for some reason. Once in a store, she wanted to see a cute child. She bent over and got right in his face to see him better and yelled hello! This startled the kid and his mom. She meant no harm, and no harm was done. I probably shouldn't laugh, but it was funny!

We eventually moved his mom to assisted living, and then to a nursing home where she died from Alzheimer's. Her death hit my husband hard of course. He had a very special experience scattering her ashes in the Sandias. Two ravens appeared and circled over his head. Then a third one joined. They continued to circle over him, then flew away. My husband always felt a connection to ravens. They are his totem (spirit animal). In some cultures, it's believed that ravens carry spirits on their wings to the afterlife. He liked to think his father and brother came to get his mom and take her home. Absolutely beautiful!

We were navigating life together great! What a team! Over the years, we pursued many sports and hobbies including scuba diving, shooting sporting clays, mountain biking, golfing, fly fishing, skiing and kayaking. We traveled and camped all over the Four Corners area, enjoying the unique beauty of each state, which are NM, CO, AZ, and UT. We loved to hike and ski in the backcountry, and our dogs joined us often. We took wonderful vacations to beautiful scuba diving destinations where we included other fun activities such as ziplining and deep-sea fishing. We traveled to Alaska and San Juan Island to sea kayak. We visited the many glorious National Parks and Monuments in the west. We were each other's favorite playmate! We were weekend warriors and were hardly ever home. We were either traveling, or out enjoying a sport or two. There's just so much to see and do!

I can't write about all the amazing things we've seen and done, because it would be too much! However, I do have a few adventures that stand out to share.

My stand-out scuba diving adventure involved large blacktip sharks. We were diving at a dive site that was near another dive site where sharks are fed to provide the shark experience for divers. The sharks are called in by banging on air tanks. We didn't know this. Towards the end of our dive my husband, me, and one other man were the only ones that still had air in our tanks, and we were hanging out on the reef not far from the boat. I banged on my air tank to get my husband's attention to show him something. Out of nowhere, six large blacktip sharks came swimming towards us! It was dreamlike, like from out of a fog. We were a little nervous and closed the gap between us. The other man was farther away and stopped to watch. The sharks were swimming all around us! I looked down to see a large eight-foot shark pass just beneath me! I didn't know their heads are square from above! They are very elegant swimmers with their smooth, slow, quiet, side-to-side motion. It was spellbinding to watch them. The sharks must've decided they weren't going to get fed and they disappeared, back into the fog. I'm surprised I wasn't scared. I loved it! The experience was surreal, and one to treasure! The other divers on the boat were jealous and disappointed that they'd missed seeing the sharks.

My stand-out sporting clays adventure is what I'll call the trophy year. We did so many different sports and activities for fun that it made it hard to excel at any one thing, which was okay with us. One year we decided to dedicate more time to train for, and compete in, sporting clays tournaments. We did well and went to the regional championship competition in Colorado. On the first meet-and-greet night we made friends with a nice couple and their lady friend. We all hung out together for the two-day tournament. Everyone shot very well and at the end of the tournament, our table was full of trophies! The other man in the group won overall champion, my husband won first place in the hunters' division, and the three of us ladies won first, second, and third place in the women's division! I placed third. Our new friends were impressive and inspiring to watch. The course was the most difficult we'd seen, and we were up against some tough competition. I'm not competitive generally but winning third place was a prideful and exciting feeling! I was excited for all of us!

My stand-out sea kayaking adventure involved an Orca whale. We were on San Juan Island to sea kayak and hopefully see some Orca whales. There are three resident Orca pods (families) that live there year-round. Orca sightings are not guaranteed, and many people never get to see them, as the ocean is so large. Over the course of a few days, we had not one, or two, but three amazing close encounters with Orcas, all from kayaks. Lucky us! I told everyone in the group we were kayaking with that it was because I'd been praying to the Orca gods, which I had. I told them to expect to see Orcas at ten o'clock on our last morning together. They didn't know I was kidding, and people were checking their watches and looking for Orcas to appear at ten. So funny! Wouldn't that have been so cool if it worked? One special day we paddled to the southern tip of the island, then turned around to head back. My husband and I were the last to turn around along with one guide. We were looking back and talking with the guide when we saw an Orca surface and dive right underneath her kayak! The Orca rolled onto her side, with her dorsal fin underwater, and glided alongside of our kayak! We watched the large white patch on her black body pass by. She seemed to pass by in slow motion. She was so close to us that I saw her eye, as she was watching me, watching her! Time stood still in that instant. I was in awe at being so close! I turned to my husband and asked, did that just happen? It was fascinating that the kayak didn't move at all! You would think we'd be tipped over, but it was still instead - amazing!

My stand-out skydiving adventure is also my only one. We took the course to learn how to skydive, which was fun and exciting. On our first jump, my husband had just left the plane and I was the last student to leave the plane. When I started to exit the plane onto the small platform beneath the wing, I was unprepared for the force of the wind. I brought my legs back into the plane. My instructors' eyes got wide, and she was worried. I assured her I was just mentally recalibrating my exit to be more aggressive.

We left the plane three thousand feet above the ground. Our parachutes were tethered to the plane to pull out for us when we jumped, which is required on your first jump. My parachute didn't open all the way because my lines were tangled. I kept my cool and I employed my training and kicked this way and that way until I untangled the lines, and the shoot opened all the way. Whew! The jump was everything I'd dreamed of. I was flying! I could see forever as I turned in all directions. I loved it! The fascinating thing about skydiving is how the wind blows *up* your body as you fall gently towards the ground. There's only one way to experience that. We were on one-way radios with the instructor on the ground so he could guide us and tell us when to flare our chutes to, hopefully, land softly on the ground. Unfortunately, the instructor misjudged our decent and told both of us to flare too soon. We both dropped from too high, and crash landed. We weren't hurt, because our training included learning how to roll when you hit the ground. Sadly, it wasn't the graceful landing I had pictured in my mind. Darn it! We intended to return for more jumps, but we never did. My husband realized he didn't like the inability to self-rescue. If your chute fails, that's it! Plus, skydiving for two people was too expensive for us to pursue. I'm so happy I had at least one chance to enjoy skydiving!

One of my early accounting jobs was at an aviation business that provided chartered flights and air ambulance services. I loved working there. I worked with a man whose job was to coordinate and dispatch the planes, pilots, and medical crews for air ambulance emergencies. He always had a two/way radio on him and was on call 24/7, which made for a very stressful job. Yet, he whistled when he walked, had a kind smile, and I never once saw him agitated or stressed. It seemed he'd found the secret to happiness. He was a good role model. He carried a coffee cup with an Osar Wilde quote on it that read:

"Life is too important to take seriously."

When airplanes get repaired or have routine maintenance done, a check flight is required before it's put back in service. My pilot friends would let me join them on these check flights because I love flying. The flights made my husband worry, and he didn't want to know about them until afterward. He wanted me to keep secrets from him!

My husband was an automotive mechanic, a very good one with a loyal following. My accounting career was going well, but I knew that it would be better if I added the letters C-P-A after my name (Certified Public Accountant). I needed a few more accounting college credits to sit for the CPA exam, so I took a couple of classes. Then, I took a prep course and studied all summer for the exam. The exam has four parts and hundreds of questions, and it requires two full days to take. The exam was held at one location for all participants and was supervised and timed. Calculators weren't allowed to avoid cheating, so I had to learn how to do math long-hand fast. I would practice by taking the phone book and adding, subtracting, multiplying, and dividing phone numbers. Ugh! I passed all four parts on my first try and got my CPA license in 1991. Three hundred of us took the test then. Only twelve of us passed all four parts because that's how hard it is! This is one of my proudest achievements!

I was laid off from a job in 1992 when the company was acquired by another company. I decided to startup a CPA business in Edgewood at age thirty-one. I had the CPA license; I might as well use it! I served as the Treasurer of the Edgewood Chamber of Commerce to become more connected with the community. After five years, I sold my CPA business because I'd had it with tax season! Preparing taxes was a significant part of my business and the heavy workload in the first few months of each year was absurd! That's no way to live. If you use a tax preparer, be kind to them. After I sold my business, I moved from job to job over the years pursuing higher responsibilities with higher pay, and that worked out well for me.

Speaking of tax season, why on earth does everyone in America have to file taxes at the same time in April!? How about basing tax filing deadlines on our birthday months? How about a flat tax rate system that would be as effective, more efficient and fairer than the difficult, overly complicated mess we have now? A girl can dream, right?

I'm grateful for my entrepreneurial experience. I enjoyed my clients and the freedom to be my own boss. One of my clients was an attorney and I rented his conference room from him to meet with my clients. He belonged to a large waterskiing club and one summer he invited my husband and I to join in the fun. We had a blast that summer waterskiing, camping at the lake with our dogs and enjoying our new friends. Fun in the sun! I learned how to slalom ski, which is on one ski. There was a big competition at the end of the summer with a course on the lake that was made of several floating buoys spread out in two parallel lines. The boat raced down the middle, and the skier tried to ski around alternating buoys from both lines. I competed in the women's slalom division. I wasn't very good on one ski yet, so I went straight down the middle behind the boat! I wasn't competing to win, just having fun. As it turned out, I was the only woman who didn't fall in the course, so I won first place! Ha! I was ceremoniously awarded a gold medal on a ribbon around my neck. That gave us all a good laugh!

I love photography very much. I took a photography class in high school and learned how to take and print black and white photos, which was fun! My stepmom was a wonderful photographer, and she printed her own photos. She knew I had a passion for photography and when she and dad sold their house and moved, she gave me all her darkroom equipment. That same year, my husband gave me some great books about black and white photography for Christmas, and we built a darkroom for me. My photo hobby just became a whole lot more fun!

The next thing I know, I'm investing in cameras and lenses, different filters, photo paper of all varieties and sizes, and all kinds of cool camera and darkroom paraphernalia. For me, upgrading camera gear is essential as it continually improves, which is fun! Later in my life when I converted from film to digital photography, I invested in photo printers and photo software. And when we moved, we built another darkroom for me. I spent hours in my darkroom trying different techniques to make the perfect print. Sometimes to the point of obsession, like when my husband knocked on the darkroom door to let me know dinner was almost ready. He knocked again to let me know my dinner was getting cold. He came back later to tell me it was late, and he was going to bed. He was amused by this because he knew I was having a good time.

In 1995, I joined the Albuquerque Photo Club which had one-hundred members at the time. I learned a great deal about photography through the monthly presentations and the competitions that were judged and critiqued. I went on fun photo adventures with fun photographer friends. I made a life-long best friend from that club. We had an immediate connection, as if we'd known each other all our lives. He and his wife became some of our best friends. His photo style includes interesting abstracts, which are great! At one point he was the President of the photo club, and I was the Vice-President. We bought a set of studio lights together and I learned how to shoot studio portraits. I've enjoyed shooting dozens of portraits in studios and outdoors ever since then. One year I had a great time shooting portraits of friends at a New Year's Eve party. Everyone got all dressed up and I set up the studio lights and a backdrop in our friend's garage! I also learned to how to do wedding photography. Over the years, I enjoyed photographing a dozen weddings. To me, there's no one more beautiful than a bride on her wedding day.

I'm the only person I know who still makes photo albums. I have thirty-nine photo albums and counting. I write down dates, places and names next to the photos. My life is captured in photo journals going back to high school. My husband and mom had cameras and enjoyed photography, too. They preferred to use the simpler point-and-shoot camera. Mom photographed people at family parties and made extra prints for us, which I cherish! My husband's style was different from mine, and I love his photos! I'm particular about which photos go into the albums. I choose only the greatest hits! My superpower is organizing things. Each album is labeled by consecutive numbers and dates. I keep a log of the contents in each album in a spreadsheet so I can easily look up and find something specific like a travel destination or an event. I love my photo albums! They are a lot of fun to make and a wonderful way to reminisce. Photography is the ultimate hobby!

Fun Fact: Mom's dad and maternal grandfather were both photographers and printed their own photos, too! One of my most cherished photos is a portrait of my mom in high school, taken and printed by her dad. This image is my great-grandfather in 1905. It's a postcard with a note written in Danish on the back. Pretty cool!

My oldest niece had a beautiful baby girl in 1997. I went straight to being a *great*-aunt! She was born twelve weeks premature. I could hold her tiny body, from neck to bottom, in one hand! She had a rough start; she overcame it, and she grew into a lovely woman. My older sister, the grandma, made a halo and some angel wings for her to wear for a black and white photo shoot we did when she was one. My niece and great-niece played and laughed and laughed that day. They never seemed to stop giggling. They still giggle a lot. We had a great time, and the photos are so adorable! My two beautiful grandmothers became great-great-grandmothers. There were five generations all living at one time and in the same place in Albuquerque!

While living in NM, my husband and I enjoyed many fun friends. We met interesting and fun people with a passion for whatever sport we shared. Trivia night and Superbowl parties became a tradition. Another tradition was the Christmas cookie parties. In the right company, decorating Christmas cookies can be hilarious! One couple, some of our best friends, had get-togethers often to enjoy margaritas and good times. My husband and the other man were the best storytellers! They could make you laugh until your stomach aches.

After fifteen years, we fell out of love with Albuquerque. The population, crime, and violence were escalating, especially the road rage. I did not want to die on the streets of Albuquerque! It was time to move away. We traveled to Durango throughout the years to hike, kayak, mountain bike, and ski, so my husband thought it would be a great place to live. I said, been there done that, let's go find another place like Durango. We traveled around the western and northwestern states. We found many beautiful mountain towns, with a river running through them, that were similar to Durango. But in the end, there's only one Durango. No sooner had we made the decision to move to Durango when an accounting job in Durango appeared in the paper. I applied and was hired on the spot. I gave my two weeks' notice at my old job, moved to Durango, and started working at my new job. Whew! That was fast! My husband stayed behind and packed the house while I looked for a place to live in Durango.

Just before we moved to Durango, my mom's husband died. He was eighty. He was twenty years older than her, and they were married for fifteen years. He was in the hospital with pneumonia and ended up on machines that were keeping him alive. Several weeks went by, and Mom and her three stepdaughters eventually had to decide to pull the plug on the machines. Absolutely the right decision, but intensely difficult to make! Those were dark days for Mom, and I didn't know how to relieve her heartbreak and suffering. About ten of us joined together at the hospital to support each other and send him on his way. It's one of the hardest things to ever have to do! He was a war veteran, and his ashes were placed in the military cemetery with a memorial service in Santa Fe.

Mom was devastated! It was hard for us to move away and leave her at that time. Before we moved away, several of us helped Mom move into a smaller place and she settled in there with her poodles. I called her often and visited when I could. Mom was close to her oldest stepdaughter who visited and helped her a lot. I'm very grateful to her for being there for my mom. After about four years, mom's stepdaughter talked her into answering a personal ad. Mom ended up meeting and marrying her fourth husband. This turned her life around. She had been depressed, but also strong enough to carry on. He told her jokes to make her laugh. Mom always loved a good joke. He took care of her, and she took care of him.

We suffered another loss just before we moved. Our sweet yellow labrador died after a good, long life. Losing our beloved dogs is so hard on the heart! I really wish dogs lived longer. We added a handsome red labrador to the family to keep our red husky company. They were quite a pretty pair and best buddies. Our husky finally had a buddy who loved to play! The small, young lab pup would grab the leash on the large, older husky with his teeth and walk him around. Hilarious!

Chapter Five

Married Life in Colorado

2000 to 2010

Moving to Durango was the best decision ever! This was in 2000. We rented a place west of Durango for a few months. Then, we bought our house on five acres east of Durango. We had an opportunity to buy the adjoining five-acre lot as a package. We scraped together the money for it and sold the adjoining lot a year later for a nice profit. We kept our home in Edgewood and rented it out for a year. Then we sold it for a small profit. Mobile homes aren't real-estate investments. However, it was cheap, paid off, and we basically lived in NM rent-free for fifteen years!

Durango life was the perfect fit for us! Durango is a sports town full of outdoor and adventurous people like us. The four corners area is truly one of the most beautiful places on earth! We were always out exploring the endless opportunities to enjoy this awesome, gorgeous planet.

My first job in Durango ended after just three months; it was my choice. Things were unacceptable there. I struggled with that decision, and I even cried. It was risky to quit without another job lined up. We'd just moved, and we had a house to pay for! We both agreed that some things are more important, such as choosing what we will or won't tolerate. We knew we would be okay. Leaving that job was a blessing because the next job was great! I did the same thing at another job many years later. I left due to unacceptable circumstances, without another job lined up, and it worked out for the best then, too.

If you trust that you will land on your feet, you will!
It's important to trust yourself and choose what's best for you.

I'd had a difficult year, so my husband treated me to a flight in a glider for my anniversary present. While waiting for my turn to go up, we noticed that people had the biggest smiles on their faces when they got out of the glider. I was about to find out why. A glider is a small plane with two seats, long wings, and no motor. It's pulled up into the sky by a plane with a motor and then detached to fly solo. It's an odd experience to feel the thermals that lift the plane to help it gain altitude. Flying in the glider was unexpectedly very quiet, and the scenery was that much prettier as we flew close to the hills and mountains in the beautiful Animas Valley. It turns out that customers have the option to make large end-over loops near the airstrip and experience G-forces (gravitational forces) if that appeals to them. Yes, please! Oh my God! One instant, you're staring at the sky, and the next, you're staring at the ground! The G-force presses you against the seat and takes over your body. We had enough altitude to do two loops.

G-force loops are a wild and crazy, super fun rush! Very exciting! And that's why everyone is smiling from ear to ear when they get out of the glider.

We made some friends quickly through my new job when we joined a group of coworkers, spouses, and partners of different ages who got together often for Friday beers, good times, and laughter. The original group was twelve to sixteen people. The group size decreased over time, but a core group remained and continued the tradition for a dozen years! One of the friends' daughters called us the Nerd Herd, and the nickname stuck. We all became good friends and did many fun things together, besides drinking beers and laughing, like hiking and backcountry skiing.

Durango became an even more perfect place to live when, a year after we moved there, my dad and stepmom moved to Durango, too! My younger sister and her family were living right across the border in Farmington, NM, and my younger brother and his family lived a few hours away in Divide, Colorado. Eventually, they all moved to Durango as well! I never would have guessed it! This has been a great blessing for all of us. *Fun Fact:* My younger brother is a very talented musician, and I've been a fan all along. He plays many instruments with different bands and plays for fun, lots of fun!

We live where the deer and elk roam. It's a treat to see the spotted baby deer in the summer. We enjoy four distinct seasons. Ravens and geese are here year-round. Eagles, Hawks, vultures, and blue herons can be seen occasionally. Mockingbirds show up in the spring and serenade us with their creative songs, which are formed from multiple other bird songs. Hummingbirds entertain everyone all summer. A variety of other beautiful birds come and go. Jackrabbits are very playful, spring high into the air, and perform crazy moves. Cottontail bunnies are speedy little critters who always run in a stop-n-go or zig-zag pattern. Lizards are curious and will hang out with you.

We have expansive views of the La Plata Mountains to the west, and the sunsets from our deck are spectacular! The sky is filled with stars on clear nights. The southwest landscape is full of surprises, which makes each year unique. The colorful cactus blooms are very cheery. The fields of wildflowers in the mountains are unbelievably beautiful! I love it here!

Admittedly, not everything about living in the country is great, such as being startled awake in the middle of the night by the coyotes' high-pitched screams to alert the pack when they've made a kill. The worst thing is a mouse in the house, which is unacceptable. Then there are the skunks, pee-ewe! And we have mud season to deal with.

Over the years, my career has become better than I could've ever dreamed of! I worked for some great companies. I traveled for work to Sydney, Australia; Montreal, Canada; New York City and Washington, DC. I flew around the southwest in a private company plane. Who knew accounting could be so much fun!? Many challenges came my way. I rose to meet them all, and I was well paid, but not as well paid as a man!

Three of the companies I worked for were international. I made friends in the places I just mentioned, plus the UK, Germany, and Israel. I've learned through these friendships that we may be from different areas of the world with different cultures and backgrounds, but we all share basic similarities.

We are all human, and no two humans are alike.
Look around, and you'll see what I mean.

I don't identify people as this or that, just us. Sadly, humans build borders and many other ways within the borders to separate Us from Them. This separation is built on fear-based ideologies and passes from generation to generation. Here's the truth: there is no Us and Them! We are all one! These fear-based ideologies also create a world of the Have and the Have-nots. Here's another truth: there's enough for everyone!

This is a story about my brief brush with fame. For my fortieth birthday, we went to Las Vegas, NV, with our good friends from Albuquerque. We were walking through one of the tunnels that connect hotels when we came across the open back of a stage, where a band was playing for an audience. We stopped to watch. To our surprise, the lead singer was a famous professional basketball player! He saw us and came towards us. He was a seven-foot-tall black man with flaming red hair, wearing black leather, and had many piercings. He came down the stairs and straight over to me. He held his microphone for me to sing along with the song they were playing. I looked way up at him and swallowed hard. Fortunately, I knew the song and did my best singing, which isn't saying much. I may have thrown in a dance move. At the end of the song, he wanted me to follow him onto the stage. I didn't want to, so I shook my head. He bent way over and gave me a shoulder hug, smiled, and returned to the stage. That was crazy! We all laughed! My husband joked that it was a good thing that went well because he and the other man in the group decided, based on the size of the guy, that I was on my own. Gee, thanks a lot.

There's a saying which is - 'Into each life some rain must fall.' Well, sometimes it's a storm! I rarely get sick. Unfortunately, in 2004, at age forty-two, I got very, very sick. On the fourth of July, after spending the day four-wheeling in our jeep, I had a terrible headache that became so bad we went to the emergency room. A CT scan showed what looked like an inoperable tumor on my brain. My husband

and family were told that I may not survive the night. How devastating!

I was heavily sedated on morphine and had no idea what was going on. My stepmom shared with me that a clergywoman visited me and asked me if I was afraid to die. I don't remember it. Apparently, I said, no, I wasn't afraid to die. That's because I'm not. We all die. It's how we transition back home, from my point of view. What is there to be afraid of? To be honest, it's something I look forward to, when it's my time. I believe there's something unbelievable and unimaginable waiting for us, and it will be a grand adventure to find out what it is.

I was put on IV antibiotics and flown to a hospital in Santa Fe, where they did a brain MRI and a spinal tap. What I had was an abscess (infection pocket) on my brain, not a tumor, and I had bacterial spinal meningitis. I had dental work done recently and the infection was caused by a common mouth bacterium. How I got the infection could not be proven, but I'm certain it could only be one thing.

It's a fact that dental work can cause serious infections that could become deadly.

After learning this the hard way, I began taking single-dose fast-acting antibiotics whenever I went to the dentist to prevent infections, and so did my husband. I also found a new dentist.

Everyone in my loving family who could travel to Santa Fe did. It was a scary time for us all. Everyone was there to support me and each other. I was on strong pain medication for my headache 24 hours a day. As soon as the medication wore off, I needed more. We were not impressed with the neurologist and the medical doctor (MD). The neurologist seemed too busy for me. He stopped in to talk to us only one time. We were surprised he could fit his large ego into the room. After a week, the MD held my second brain MRI up to the window and said he wasn't a radiologist, but the abscess looked smaller to him, and he sent me home. Seriously!? I wasn't doing any better. I was released from the hospital in Santa Fe on IV antibiotics and directed to get another brain MRI in ten days.

My stepmom and younger sister are both MDs, and they were shocked when I was sent home. The minute we got back home, my husband took my brain MRIs to my sister, who immediately took them to a neurologist she knew well in Farmington, NM, for a second opinion. He told her to get me in to see him immediately. We saw him the next morning. He'd determined from the MRIs we gave him that the abscess had grown! He'd already scheduled the operating room for three o'clock that afternoon. I needed immediate brain surgery to save my life! The abscess needed to be drained before it burst, which would be deadly. It was located next to my right ventricle, and if it burst, my entire body would become septic instantly, and nothing could be done to save me if that happened. Those were the scariest words I've ever heard! I wasn't ready to die yet! The neurologist asked if I would consent to the surgery. I said, where do I sign! We had some time before the surgery and went for a stroll around the hospital. My husband was rolling me down a hospital hallway in a wheelchair when we hit a small bump, and I bounced a little. We gasped! Not so funny at the time, but we laughed about it later. The surgery was successful, and I was released from the hospital a week later, and my long road to recovery began.

The treatment to fight the infection lasted for two-and-a-half months. I had a wonderful infectious disease doctor and his staff, who got me through the treatment. I had an IV port on the inside of my upper left arm that went into my heart. I had to do IV drips from a bag three times a day, 6AM, 2PM, and 10PM, every day for ten weeks! I had to get many brain MRIs, which are very stressful. MRI machines are too closed in, and they take too long! It was a tight fit in there, and my face was just inches from the ceiling. They put a cage over my head to keep it still! I kept my eyes squeezed shut and took deep breaths to stay calm. I never, ever want to get another MRI! I was sick and depleted from the infection, antibiotics, and anesthesia. I was on anti-seizure medication, so I couldn't drive. I was unable to go into the office to work, so they set me up to work remotely from home.

Thankfully, I'm a natural-born optimist, and I remained upbeat for the most part. I believed that I would get better and that it was only a matter of time. Still, there were times when I cried. When I was young, my mom called me her little Pollyanna from the storybook. I didn't know the Pollyanna story, but I could tell it must be a good thing because she hugged me and smiled. Later in life, I read the story. Pollyanna is a young girl who sees the best in people and looks on the bright side of things. Mom's comment stays in my heart because it's how she saw me.

When life gets hard, look around at the many things there are to be grateful for. Things could be better, but more importantly, things could be worse!

Several weeks into the treatment, we got the news we were waiting for! The abscess was completely gone! The neurologist told us he couldn't find anything in my brain MRI. Nothing, really? It just didn't sound right when you put it that way. I still had the spinal meningitis to beat, which I did. I am forever indebted to my surgeon and my doctor; they are my heroes! Saying thank you felt so inadequate. I gave them each a black and white photo I took, printed, and framed especially for them. I knew what to give each one based on conversations we'd had. I signed them with Thank You in capital letters. I learned years later that my surgeon canceled his vacation to save me.

The love and support of my husband, family, and friends was the most healing medicine of all! My coworkers brought me cards, flowers, and a soft, cuddly care bear named Bearnard. I appreciated having Bearnard at the hospital to hug in the middle of the night when it was dark and scary. We bonded, and he's lived on my dresser ever since. My husband would go home after work, feed the dogs, then drive an hour each way to visit me. I told him he didn't have to, but he wouldn't be talked out of it. Thank goodness! He lit up the room every time he walked in, and I needed it. We've learned that the only way to get through the hardships in life is to keep putting one foot in front of the other. I call them endurance tests. By October, we were high in the mountains, enjoying stunning views of endless mountain ranges and celebrating the end of my treatments and my health returning.

Nothing nurtures like nature!

I want to stress that my case was badly mishandled at the hospital in Santa Fe. If we had waited those ten days as originally directed, I could've died! I reported the neurologist and MD to the NM State Medical Board. As expected, the board did nothing, but it did go on their record, which is something. I reported them because I want them to learn from this and never do it again! My sister's actions saved my life, and she's my hero, too!

Let this be a warning to anyone with a medical condition.
It's important to have an advocate and to get a second opinion.

We celebrated our twentieth wedding anniversary in 2005 and had a custom anniversary ring made for me as my present. My husband's wedding ring was stolen years before from his toolbox at work, which totally sucked! Especially because it was originally his brother's wedding ring. He said he didn't want a new one. Whoever stole his ring is very lucky my husband didn't find them. I designed my beautiful ring, and it has a gorgeous golden topaz stone, which is my birthstone, the diamond from my wedding ring, and inlaid turquoise and malachite. I secretly had a beautiful custom ring made for my husband. It was a simple band with inlaid turquoise and malachite. The extra special touch was his initials set in tiny letters on either side of the ring. He was very surprised; he loved it very much, and he was deeply moved. That was the nicest gift I ever gave to anyone, and it felt soooo good!

Tragically, in 2009, my mom lost her battle with diabetes. She was seventy. I was devastated! I cried uncontrollably! Damn, it hurts to lose the ones you love so much! A few months later, friends and family gathered in NM to celebrate her life. I prepared a hand-out for the guests about her and her life, which was a healing process, and it felt right. I read my eulogy with smiles, not tears. I was able to truly celebrate her life with her friends and our family because my heart was where it needed to be on that day - filled with love. Mom was always my best friend and my biggest fan. She was smart, kind, thoughtful and caring. She was a beautiful woman, inside and out. I wish so much that we could've had more time together! I miss her!

Did I mention how smart my husband was yet? He's one of the smartest people I've ever known. He enjoyed reading about anything and everything. I called him a readaholic and a magazine junkie. He could discuss any topic with any person. He knew so much about so much! He was my walking and talking encyclopedia and he taught me many things. My dad is a brilliant man. He's a nuclear physicist. They both loved to debate. My dad was a champion debater in high school and college and my husband was just naturally good at debating. He debated with anyone for personal entertainment. They had great debates together, just for fun! My stepmom and I would just sit and watch them. The topics were way over our heads! Never underestimate your auto mechanic! *Fun Fact*: My dad was one of three partners that invented the first nuclear radiation detection device, it's called a Giger counter, and it's still in use today!

**Never underestimate anyone.
Everyone has a story.**

Sadly, our red husky died after a good long life. He held the record of sixteen years! We were relieved that our red lab seemed perfectly content to be an only child. Our hearts were broken again, and we didn't have it in us to add another family member.

My husband and I both rode motorcycles and lived in a beautiful place to enjoy them. I learned what the freedom of the open road is all about. Riding a motorcycle is an exciting, fun, sumptuous, and intimate way to experience the environment, and the sky is huge! I would cheer at the top of my lungs while riding through incredible, picturesque scenery. Of course, no one could hear me because I wore a helmet. As much as I loved riding, I feared getting hit by a car that didn't see me. Most of our riding was out on highways, and we stayed close together in towns to be safe. When I almost hit a motorcycle that I didn't see, that was the end for me. I very reluctantly sold my motorcycle after six years of riding adventures. I cherish the thousands of miles of fun we had, and I feel lucky that nothing bad happened. I still crack a smile when I hear my neighbor fire up his motorcycle because I love that sound!

Unfortunately, it turns out that the cancer treatments back in the 1980s have consequences. The radiation treatments sometimes resulted in heart disease years later. Soon after Mom's life celebration in 2009, we were hiking in western Colorado when my husband felt severe pain in his back under his left shoulder blade. We stopped, and he took off his backpack. We were up on the highest point of the trail and halfway through a ten-mile hike. The pain passed, and he was able to continue for the rest of the hike. When he was walking the dogs a couple of days later, the severe pain in his back happened again, and it dropped him to his knees. We went to the emergency room. They found that he had three severely clogged arteries to his heart! He needed triple bypass surgery and a possible aortic valve replacement. What!? He'd been so healthy for twenty years, and now this!?

He was flown to the heart hospital in Albuquerque at noon on a Friday. My younger sister and I drove there, fast! The surgeon determined that the surgery could wait until Monday, and the surgery team would have the weekend to rest. We met with the surgeon to discuss the situation. We were thankful to have a surgeon who was one of the best in his field, and we were grateful to my sister for coming with us. We all agreed that scheduling the surgery for the first surgery on Monday morning was a good plan. Our Albuquerque friends and family visited us at the hospital. They let us bring beer and enchiladas to the hospital room. My husband was feeling fine, so we had a party! Enjoying time with friends was much better than dwelling on things.

His surgery was successful, but having your chest cracked open is no joke. They had him get out of bed on the same day as his surgery. My sister said it was like climbing Mt. Everest for him to do that. The surgeon determined during his surgery that his aortic valve did not need to be replaced right then. My husband was a physically fit man, and he pushed through his recovery relatively quickly, though it wasn't easy. He worked with a personal trainer, and she has a rare gift for healing damaged bodies. Soon, my very tough husband, who never complained, was back in action. The aortic valve was still a concern as it would most likely need to be replaced someday. It scares me to think of what could've happened way out there on the trail that day.

Chapter Six

Getting Older

2011 to 2016

I wasn't happy about turning fifty at first. I was getting old, right? Then, I thought about all the women I knew between the ages of forty-five and sixty-five, and I thought, we look damn good! Age really is just a number. What matters more is being young at heart. I decided to celebrate this, and I created the 'Young-Heart-Ladies-Club.' I rented out one-half of a wine bar and invited twenty women to join the club and come celebrate with me. They all came. It was a lot of fun, and I think we all had a great time. I know I did! Women are amazing and awesome! It's not like me to throw a party for myself, but I'm so happy I did!

Being an auto mechanic for so long was taking its toll on my husband, and it was time to stop. Fortunately, we could afford to live on my salary. Lucky for me, I became a totally spoiled woman! Not working was hard on my husband's ego, so he insisted on taking over all the life stuff for both of us. Our marriage had always been an equal partnership of sharing life stuff. He became a good cook even though neither of us liked cooking very much. He did all the cooking, cleaning, shopping, and whatever chores and errands needed doing. I pitched in from time to time to give him a break. Oh yeah, and I did my own laundry. Boy, did I love being spoiled!

My favorite aunt and uncle (mom's brother) lived in NM. They were always a part of my life. They were outdoor dogs like us and fun people to spend time with. In 2011, at age seventy-two, my uncle lost his battle with Parkinson's disease. They were married for forty-six years and were soul mates. The last few years were very hard ones, and my aunt did an amazing job caring for him. His death was very sad but also a blessing. I will always remember his funny humor, laughter, and smile. We were happy to have my aunt visit us any time she could, especially during the holidays.

In 2012, our handsome red labrador died after a good, long life. Geez! I can't take it anymore! Not that we would've changed a thing. All our dogs were beautiful, athletic, smart, and great companions. This red lab became the strongest and most athletic dog. Once on a trail, just for fun, he leaped across boulders in the creek, then ran swiftly up and down the side of the hill over fallen trees and rough terrain, then ran back to us across the creek over logs and rocks. He accomplished this with ease and grace, and he didn't miss a step! Another time, he accidentally fell into a fast-moving highwater creek. My husband jumped in after him, but he was swept away by the strong current. He swam hard against the current and got behind a protruding rock on the other side of the creek. He swam hard again towards us to another rock. Then he swam hard again to the bank. My husband raced down the side of the creek and pulled him to safety. Whew! Thank God he was such a strong swimmer! I don't know any other dog who could pull that off.

A year after we lost our labrador, we felt something was missing from our lives, and we decided to open our hearts one last time. We adopted a rare Korean Jindo from the Animal Humane Society. He was one year old and knew basic commands. Another beautiful, athletic, smart, great companion. How did we keep getting so lucky? Jindo's look like a husky, but all white with some red mixed in. He has the cutest white eyelashes on his pretty brown eyes. He presented a new challenge for us. Jindo's are bred to hunt and to protect. That meant we had to keep him contained at all times, either on a leash or in a fenced yard.

My husband once said that as long as this dog was around, he would not worry about my safety. The only time he barks is to sound an alarm, and it's alarming!

Our Jindo became my great little protector, which is a blessing and a curse. He'll take down any dog that comes close to me. He never seriously hurts them; he just makes them submit. He was just doing his job, after all. This made things difficult with all the loose dogs on the trails. Eventually, I had to limit the places he could go. He's great with people, and once I've greeted them, he loves everyone, and everyone loves him! My husband did a great job training this dog.

This Jindo became the smartest dog in terms of his vocabulary; it's extensive! I talk to him in full sentences, and he understands what I'm saying. I swear, it's true! He's wicked smart. I spell words, like w-a-l-k, when talking to someone so he doesn't think we're going for a walk. I wouldn't be surprised if he learns how to spell too!

In 2013, my husband became eligible for an aortic valve replacement. What makes you eligible is the degradation of the aortic valve to a certain point. The surgery wasn't necessary yet, but it would be eventually. He decided to voluntarily have the valve replaced. He did not want to wait until he was old and go through another open-heart surgery. He was fifty-five. We had to choose between a biological or mechanical valve. There were pros and cons to both. We chose the mechanical option, which meant being on blood thinner medication for the rest of his life. This is the con. The pro is the guarantee that it would last for the rest of his life. Biologic valves sometimes must be replaced, meaning a potential third surgery.

We traveled to the Mayo Clinic in Minnesota for his second open-heart surgery. He prepared for months ahead of time, working out with his gifted personal trainer. One of our best friends went with us for support. She was a valued blessing, and it made all the difference to have her there. The surgery was successful. His recovery wasn't easy, however, his efforts to prepare in advance paid off and he was back doing what he loves to do within months, including a scuba diving vacation to Hawaii later that year. He did what had to be done and never complained - again. Everyone who knew him well knew what a strong man he was.

We had a stand-out adventure in Kauai, HI. We bought powered hang-glider lessons for an hour and a half. These are large kites with two seats and a propeller. We each had a kite and pilot. As students, we got instructions during the flight. We had headphones and microphones to talk with the pilots. We took off and flew with the propeller for a while, then we turned the propeller off and just flew the kite. The students get to control the kite if they want to. Heck yeah! I was flying like a giant bird with giant wings! I banked to the left, then to the right. I went up, then down. I went out over the ocean, then back over land. We were surrounded by clouds, and we could see forever! It was breathtaking! I loved seeing my husband's kite in the distance, as he was flying like a giant bird, too! I wanted to stay up there forever! Sadly, that wasn't possible. My husband landed first. When my pilot brought us in for our landing, the winds picked up suddenly, and he pulled off the landing and went back into the sky. We circled around for a second attempt, and he pulled off again. He hoped he wasn't making me nervous, and I told him I was fine. We landed safely on our third attempt. He told me that his instructor taught him that you can have as many do-overs as you want, but there's going to be only one Oh-Shit! Great advice!

In 2015, my older sister's husband died from cancer. We always cared for each other a lot, and I eulogized him at his memorial service. He lived with my oldest niece during his last years, as he and my sister were separated. My niece did a very good job caring for him, though it wasn't easy for her. My best memory of him was the Christmas in high school when he arrived carrying an adorable puppy under his arm that he gave to me. That puppy was my beautiful, amazing dog, who became my best friend. The puppy was from a litter of theirs, and my brother-in-law planned to keep him and named him. He saw how much I loved the puppy and chose to give him to me instead. Best Christmas gift ever! I'll always remember him as a good singer and a good man. He was a Vietnam War veteran, and his ashes were placed in the military cemetery in Santa Fe.

In January of 2015 my husband knew something was very wrong with his lungs and he went to the doctor. He was losing weight, swallowing food was getting harder for him, and we could hear a frightening whistle sound when he exhaled. Several months went by as he was passed from one doctor to the next. The pulmonologist kept ordering different treatments trying to find one that worked, which took months. He once told my husband he'd like to solve the problem so that my husband would stop wearing out a path in the carpet to his office. What!? I was shocked and angry when my husband told me what he said. That was a terrible thing to say!

No one diagnosed the problem, and he was getting worse. It was extremely frustrating and infuriating! We needed answers! In October we traveled to the Mayo clinic in Minnesota to get tests and answers. The first test they did was a CT scan, and he was quickly diagnosed with lung cancer! No - what!? We were devastated, and our hearts sank. This was a significant blow! I could barely think or talk. This wasn't right! Not after all he'd been through!

Unbelievably, we learned there's another potential consequence from the cancer treatments of the 1980s, which is lung cancer. My husband and I didn't smoke cigarettes. For some unknown reason, a routine CT scan was not ordered by any of the doctors in Durango. In hindsight, we wished we would've pushed to get a CT scan done the first thing, if we'd just known. There was a cancerous tumor the size of a lemon on my husband's bronchial tube which was causing serious damage. Maybe if the tumor was detected by a CT scan nine months earlier, and treated, it might not have grown larger and caused more damage. This is pure speculation, which doesn't change anything. However, it taught us a very important lesson that applies to anyone with a medical condition.

Question your doctor about tests that could be done, that aren't being done. Request tests that you want to be done.

He received three months of chemo and radiation treatments to fight the cancer. Treatments and technology have greatly improved from the 1980s. He could do both at the same time and drive himself to the treatments. The radiation oncologist was originally from Albuquerque, and he was my husband's same radiation oncologist from the 1980s! We considered this a true blessing, because he's one of the best in his field. He invited me into the control room to watch the treatment on the computer screens and explained the science behind it. Wow, it's unbelievable how much technology has changed! I was shocked to see the size of the tumor, and I thought it was huge! The oncologist said it was on the small side.

This battle was my husband's hardest battle. He withdrew from friends and family. He lost weight and all his hair. He was on a liquid diet. If the treatments worked, he had a 50/50 chance of making it five more years. If he did that, his odds would get better. He wanted those five years. I believed with all my heart that he would beat this. He was concerned I was in denial. I assured him I was not, I truly believed he would beat this. Everyone sent him and I love, prayers, and best wishes. He had so much positive energy and love surrounding him! Especially from me. I knew he was in the hardest mental battle of his life as well. He warned me we may have to have that very hard conversation. I knew what he meant, and I agreed, but only if he didn't win the battle. Well - he won the battle! The oncologist declared him to be cancer-free! He was happily surprised, but I wasn't surprised. It was mid-morning, and we stopped at a favorite bar/restaurant to drink mimosas and celebrate the great news!

He started to gain weight, grow his hair back, and eat solid food again, and he talked to a couple of buddies on the phone. One buddy told him how unfair he thought it was. My husband didn't think in terms of fairness and replied, why not me? The most endearing thing I heard him say was that he wouldn't want to be anyone else. Those were important words for me to hear and to know he felt that way.

It'd been a long, hard winter, so we traveled to Moab, UT, to enjoy some warm sunshine. We stayed at a beautiful resort on the Colorado River in the shadow of tall red cliffs. The warm sunshine and spectacular scenery were exactly what we needed. We did two easy hikes through beautiful red rock formations in Arches, NP. Nothing nurtures like nature! Eventually, he wanted to get out and socialize. We planned a dinner date with some of our best friends, who we'd been having dinner with regularly for many years.

One day, late in March 2016, it was snowing in the morning, and we had a fire in the fireplace. We made love in the afternoon. Our dinner date with friends was in a small town nearby. It was one of those wonderful evenings with friends that you don't want to end. We reminisced, told stories, and laughed a lot. They were the perfect company. My husband had his favorite meal of lamb, and he loved every bite. He said it was the lambiest lamb he ever had. Huh? After over two hours, our friends left. We decided to stay and sit in the bar, have a glass of wine, and listen to the guitarist. We were pleasantly surprised when the guitarist played two of our favorite songs that had special meanings. We drank a toast to us. We were still madly in love with each other! We left with my arm looped through his.

He didn't make it home that night... That was our last day together.

When we got to the truck, my husband coughed up some blood. The tumor damaged his bronchial tube, and we knew this was serious. I got behind the wheel, and we sped towards the hospital, which was thirty minutes away. I called 911 for an ambulance to meet us on the highway. His lungs filled with blood, and he died in less than ten minutes. I pulled over on the side of the highway and waited for the ambulance. The 911 operator was still on speakerphone and stayed with me until the ambulance arrived. I have immense respect for all the people who helped me that night. They are angels that walk upon this earth.

I called our friends we'd just had dinner with and asked them to please come get me and drive my truck home. At home, I walked in circles around the living room, repeating the words, 'I don't know what to do,' over and over. I was unable to process what happened. I needed our friends, and they were there for me. They were in shock, too. The next morning, I woke up into my worst nightmare. He was really gone. I shook my head in despair and disbelief. This can't be real! He was fifty-eight, and I was fifty-four.

Chapter Seven

The Most Profound Years

2016 to 2018

My journey into the grief process was horrible at first. I'd lost my husband and our future. It took me down to zero. My world was completely upside down. I didn't know who I was without him. For the first time in my life, I was lost, scared, and alone. I was moving slowly through dense fog on autopilot. Learning how to connect to a world and a life without him in it was my hardest battle.

There was a very scary dark hole waiting to swallow me up. Once, I was in a dark place, and I fell back onto my bed facing the ceiling with my legs dangling. I tried to move, but I couldn't. I couldn't move! It felt like I was under concrete, and it was hard to breathe! I felt paralyzed, and

I started to panic. Instead, I calmed myself down, which released its hold on me. The episode taught me that I desperately needed to heal my broken heart. I did my best to be intentional with my thoughts and not feed the dark beast. Staying positive could be as simple as making an effort to straighten my back, hold my head up, and smile as I walked. A friend who had experience with loss recommended I drink a toast to myself every night for making it through another day, which I did.

Dark energy feeds on fear and pain.
It was very important to stay positive.

My best friend stayed by my side day and night for the first few days. I've never needed a friend more! We went to Dad's house to tell him in person. I had to catch Dad when his knees buckled. Thankfully, I didn't have to tell anyone else. We had to go to the mortuary, which was too much to bear, so I threw a fit in the parking lot and refused to go inside. My friend settled me down, and we went in. I handled the process okay, and surprisingly, we even had some laughs with the owner, who had a kind, easy-going manner.

For the next many weeks my stepsister living in CA, and my aunt and best friends living in NM, all took turns visiting and caring for me. I wasn't functioning at my best. Their love, care, and help were the best things for me. After that, my aunt checked in with me daily just to make sure I was eating at least. My stepsister called me every week, a tradition that started when my husband became ill and lasted for years. In May, a good friend kindly invited me to join her on a trip north with her good friend. I didn't think I was up for it, but I said yes. It was a nice time in a beautiful place, and I'm glad I went. I said yes to invitations to hike, kayak on the lake, raft on the river, and to come for dinner. My friends and family were not going to let me just sit around. Thank you!

There were many times I wanted to say no, but saying yes instead was always the best choice.

When I returned to the mortuary by myself to pick up my husband's cremains, something special happened. I was driving home down a county road alongside a river. At the time, I was unable to listen to music with singing because too many lyrics were making me cry. I was listening to a playlist of mostly instrumental music. A song came on with singing that I let play. The simple, repeating lyrics to the beautiful Spanish guitar were "My love is always with you, so strong, so strong." I turned up the volume and sang along. I was singing and smiling and crying. I undeniably felt my husband there with me - so strong. It turned an incredibly difficult journey into a loving one.

That wasn't all that happened. The county road rises out of the river valley and opens to an expansive view of the HD Mountains to the east, which had unusual, huge clouds spreading high and wide over them, like a massive spread-out fan. The sun was setting in the west, and the clouds were lit up with bright, beautiful peach and pink colors. I could *feel* the enormous sunset! My sense of my husband grew in strength. It enveloped me and expanded beyond my imagination! My heart was overflowing with love! Time slowed down, and I slowed down, and I soaked in the experience. Later, I remembered my best friend's comment that his spirit is huge now that he's out of his battered body. That's what it felt like in that moment, and it was deeply moving.

The first three months were a blur. The world kept turning on its axis, the sun kept coming up, and I kept putting one foot in front of the other. I went to work and did my job. In July, we gathered at our house to celebrate my husband's life. My younger sister and her family were living in New Zealand at the time. They had already purchased plane tickets to visit in July, so that's why we waited. I highly recommend waiting, if possible. I needed the extra time. Maybe everyone else did, too.

Our good friends from the Nerd Herd gathered at my house, and we had a separate celebration two days before because of people's travel plans. It was nice to have everyone together again. They were a part of our lives for a long time, and having them around me made me feel good. It was a sad occasion, but we found things to laugh about as we reminisced. Many wonderful and heartfelt comments were said about my husband by people who knew him well, and I will always cherish them.

Good friends are good friends for life.

The life celebration was sad but also very special. I invited only close family and friends. Several people traveled to be there. Everyone who was there was meant to be there. I was feeling stronger by then, and when the time came to read my eulogy, I did so without any tears. What I was feeling was the immense love and gratitude I have for the life dance that we'd shared. Thank you, babe! My dad's eulogy was endearing. The death of my husband was a hard blow for Dad. He considers him one of his heroes. My husband's death was a hard blow for everyone, and we were all grieving. Everyone else spoke from their hearts. We took the time needed to share our thoughts and love. I felt like the day was mostly joyful because we were all together, celebrating and remembering him. My husband was very much loved and admired.

I have the tools and knowledge to load shotgun shells, and I still have my over-under twelve-gauge shotgun. I loaded four shotgun shells with his ashes. One of our best friends had a black powder shotgun that he filled with his ashes, too. Shooting his ashes out of those shotguns was great! It was a rush and the highlight of the day. Everyone loved it. I'm certain my husband loved it a lot! I created a slideshow of his life with over 100 photos, which was a labor of love, and everyone enjoyed it. We ended the day on my deck under the moon and stars, listening to a good friend play his wood flute. Sweet.

I had the idea to fill small, colorful envelopes with his ashes in them for anyone who wanted to take them, and they could scatter them anywhere. I made thirty envelopes, and between both celebrations, they were all taken. I made an album of all the places his ashes were scattered over the years. People sent me videos, texts, emails, and photos.

They all chose beautiful places with a special meaning. I scattered his ashes myself for five years. Every time I did, I cupped my hands around my mouth, looked up, and yelled - I Love You! The places I chose had a special meaning for us, and I also scattered his ashes in beautiful places that I knew he would love. His ashes are in seven countries, nine states, and numerous locations. What an outstanding tribute to my man!

My younger sister's talented ex-husband made the most beautiful, custom, segmented-wood urn for him. It's made with twenty-six inlaid ravens and is a work of art. Even so, I think my husband is happier outside than inside on the mantel. The beautiful wood urn has some special things in it like his anniversary ring and passports containing stamps from our travels. I would love for it to be used for my ashes, at least until they're scattered.

I posed a question to myself in the beginning. Would I rather be there with him or here without him? I very much wanted to be there, not here, at first. I wasn't suicidal, so I wasn't going anywhere. The goal was to want to be here. My response to this question over time became a way to gauge my progress. I eventually felt somewhere in the middle. Then, I finally wanted to be here.

Life is a miraculous gift, and we are all miracles.

My employer paid for a life coach for me for six months to help me cope with my grief. She became a dear friend. She said, I'm sorry you have to go through this, but you have to go through this. I was looking for the fast-forward button. She said, "Not only will you survive, but you will also thrive." I did not believe her. I couldn't imagine it. I felt like my life was over and that I could never be happy again! Through focused determination, I made peace with all of it, eventually. I became someone totally new yet still the same. A phoenix that rose from the ashes. My best friend in NM calls me version 2.0. My optimistic nature left me, but I got it back. I found joy again. People told me I was an inspiration by how I dealt with grief. It took a long time and a lot of internal work.

Everything we need to achieve our goals and be happy is inside of us. It's up to us to find it.

One analogy I used to describe grief was like being stuck circling in an eddy on the river of life. I watched life go by me, but I was unable to leave the eddy. I wanted to rejoin the river of life again someday. I also felt like I was walking through deep, thick mud. Every step was so hard! I needed to find solid ground again. Eventually, I left the eddy, and I found solid ground. I couldn't have done it without all the love and support of my wonderful family and friends. I'm extremely grateful for all the people in my life!

My aunt brought two rose bushes to the life celebration for me to plant in my yard. One for my husband and one for my mom. Thank you! The day after the celebration, I was watering them in their containers. I noticed my mom's rosebush had pink roses and rosebuds. My husband's rosebush had only one red rose that was old and falling off. There was not one single rosebud on it! I thought to myself, it's healthy, and there's still time before winter for it to bloom again. Then, *the very next day*, there was a beautiful red rose in full bloom on his rosebush! I couldn't believe it! It happened overnight! It was magic! Thanks, babe! The bush eventually filled up with roses, and it took two weeks for a rosebud to become a rose. The magic rose is saved in the wood urn, and a picture of it is the background image on my cell phone. My husband gave me, and others, many special magical gifts. Some gifts were miraculous and powerful. Other gifts, like leaving pennies for us to find, were his way of letting us know he was around. Years before, my mom also gave me some wonderful magical gifts that mean a lot to me.

One special magical gift involved ravens in flight. One morning I was having my worst meltdown. I was kicking furniture, pounding on walls, and crying out from deep inside until I was exhausted and fell into my recliner. I kept having the same repeating thought - go to the kitchen for some water, over and over, like a message. I wasn't thirsty, and I didn't want to get up. Regardless, I went to the kitchen for some water, and I noticed ravens gathering outside the window. I stepped outside onto the deck.

About thirty ravens flew in, and they filled the sky in front of me! They were circling and soaring in all directions on the gentle blowing breeze. It was a wonder they didn't collide with each other! I was captivated. After some time, they all dropped down into the trees. Three ravens popped up and did crazy moves. One did some barrel rolls, one swung back and forth like a U-shaped pendulum, and the other one dive-bombed the other two from up high, flaring its wings just before crashing into them, causing them to tumble out of the way! I didn't know ravens could do all that! I like to think it was my husband, his best friend who'd died, and his brother messing around and trying to outdo each other. Two of them dropped down into the trees, and the third one became still in the breeze, its wings out facing me. I was transfixed. Ultimately, a second raven joined it, and together, they disappeared over the hillside. The ravens lifted out of the trees and circled and soared some more. What an amazing display! Eventually, they flew away, and the show was over. I found myself laughing and clapping! It was an extraordinary experience with perfect timing, as it lifted me up when I needed it the most. It dramatically changed my mindset from excruciating pain to incredible joy. I've never seen anything like it before or since!

I figured out that having constant reminders of my husband around me would impede the healing process. The first thing I did was transform our bedroom into my oasis. I bought new furniture and drapes. I painted the walls and brought in some new art. It was a complete transformation, and I love it! I cleared out his things from the closets and bathroom. I gave away his recliner so I couldn't sit in it and cry anymore. I gave away his sports gear and other things to friends and family to enjoy and use. My brother bought his super cool motorcycle and loves it just as much as he did! I'd placed an 8x10 portrait of him on my dresser so I'd wake up to it each morning. I removed the picture from the bedroom and now I keep two of my favorite pictures of him in the guest room. Everything I did felt right to me, if it didn't feel right, I didn't do it.

It was important to the healing process to make these changes.

When life has you down, it's important to laugh. When I got very low, I would think of something funny, like the hilarious scene in the movie *Dick and Jane (2005)* when she's driving the getaway car. It always makes me laugh when I think about the scene, and laughing would shake me out of my dark mood. Watching something funny on TV is good to do. I had a favorite joke I told myself in the middle of the night when it was dark and scary. It was wonderful how laughter could improve my mood.

**Laughter truly is medicine for the heart.
Love is the greatest medicine of all.
It's most important to love yourself first.**

I did not want to share my pain or cry with my family and friends. First of all, they were hurting, too, and they worried about me. Secondly, I wanted to escape my pain by enjoying my time with them. It was important for me to have a neutral person to talk to and cry with. That was my life coach. I told her thoughts about my suffering that I didn't think I was able to share. Those thoughts would have festered in me if I didn't express them.

**It's not healthy to keep pain inside.
By letting my pain out, I could let it go.**

I described the pain of loss as if it were a giant, invisible monster that kicked me hard in the stomach and caused so much hurt and pain that I cried. Just when I started to feel a little better, it kicked me again, and I cried some more. The monster chose when to strike. I had no control over stopping the pain I felt. It was horrible! Getting kicked by the monster was especially hard in public places when it brought unwanted attention to me. Like when I was traveling alone on an airplane. I stared out the window, and I started hurting and crying. I tried to shrink, and I cried until it passed. That's all I could do. I talked about this and so much more with my life coach. Her safe space, caring words, insight, and encouragement was much needed and greatly appreciated. She has my everlasting gratitude!

I hired a family friend to deep-clean my house before the life celebration. Her husband died a few years before. She brought me a copy of a book that helped her a lot with grief. It's titled *Healing After Loss* by Martha Hickman. It's beautifully written, and I found it comforting. I've been highly recommending and gifting this unique book ever since.

The book helped me realize millions of people have walked this path before me.

My stepsister thoughtfully brought some adult coloring books and pencils when she came to visit. I was hooked on coloring right away! I have music playing in my house most of the time, and I spent hours coloring and listening to music. It was very Zen-like. The world is full of so much fantastic music to fit any mood! I also like doing puzzles and playing games on my iPad while listening to music, which is calming and relaxing. *Fun Fact:* My stepsister has a master's degree in Finance, and she lived and worked internationally. Her expertise was in the cellular phone industry, and she consulted with governments in foreign countries to introduced or improved the cellular phone industry in their countries. Impressive!

Make time to be calm and relaxed.

I started writing in a journal. Writing in my journal was very, very therapeutic. I wrote about whatever I was feeling and thinking. It was important to include the good and the bad. I wrote down sweet memories like - He loved red wine and red roses, and he rocked me when he held me. I raged and cursed like - This sucks! I asked questions, and then I'd answer myself like – Will this ever end? Yes, this will end. I sorted things out, made decisions, and I gave myself many pep talks as I filled the pages. I would occasionally go back several pages and re-read what I'd written, which helped me to see I was making progress.

I highly recommend writing in a journal!

I created a list of mantras, or positive affirmations. I would read my mantra list every day to reinforce where I wanted to be and where I needed to get back to. It grew over time, and I found inspiration everywhere. I did not believe many of these mantras when I first wrote them down. For example, I did not feel strong or know who I was or what to do. I read the mantras to myself repeatedly to help me believe again.

I highly recommend mantras!

Here's my entire mantra list:

I am Grateful and Blessed
I am Strong and Powerful
I Know who I am
I Know what to do
Be Kind and Compassionate
Be Aware and Wise
Be Tolerant and Accepting
Be Fearless and Truthful
Be Discerning and Set Boundaries
Show Respect and Command Respect
Express Love and Gratitude
Trust the Universe and Be Patient
Enjoy the Ride While it Lasts
Focus on the Positive
Keep an Open Mind
Make the Most of Each Day
Don't Put Things Off
Take Time to Just Be
Believe in Magic
LOVE is the Answer
Be at Peace that I am Where I Should Be and All is Well
I am Grounded to the Earth and Connected to the Universe
Talk to your Angels
Be a Good Listener
We Are Not Alone
Be a Light for Others

I have scoliosis, and for decades, I've been getting massages routinely to help keep my neck from locking up. After my husband died, the massages provided something I needed much more than ever before, which is the vital and basic human need for physical contact. I also make every hug a good hug! *Fun Fact:* My best friend in Durango was my massage therapist for fifteen years. She has an extraordinary gift for healing people that transcends massage. I was fortunate to be one of her clients.

I highly recommend massages!

People asked me if I would move out of our house, and I answered no. I love where I live, and I have many good neighbors. I served as the President of the Homeowners Association for ten years when we first moved in, and I've known many of my neighbors for two decades. Living here is like having a safety net.

The environment at work had become toxic. The CEO had been forcing many good people out the door for months, including my boss, which caused disruption in the workplace. We were implementing four major changes to the business model all at once, which caused stress in the workplace. We hired a replacement for my boss, who moved his family here from New York. She forced him out the door after just three months, and I was back to doing both my and my boss' jobs again.

The CEO was another person who kicked people when they were down. Two days after the life celebration, she forced me out the door. Her reasons didn't make sense.

One reason was that people felt like they needed to walk on eggshells around me, especially in the mornings. Yes, they needed to. I was fragile, especially in the mornings, and I won't apologize for that. I pressed her for the real reason she was doing this. She admitted that she'd been wanting to do it for a very long time. She explained that the only thing that stopped her until then was my boss. I guess she thought waiting until right after the life celebration was appropriate timing. I felt incredibly disrespected! It was clear to me that if I wanted a severance package, I would leave quietly. I didn't care. I was at the lowest point of my life. My former boss and I are friends, and I visited him to thank him for his support over all those years, now that I knew. We drank a beer and had a nice visit.

Losing my job was a blessing, even though it didn't seem like it at first. We'd invested in the company stock, and it was worth a lot. I sold the stock, which gave me a nice pile of cash and allowed me to take some time off. My life was filling up with activities and travels. I said yes to every invitation that came my way, as promised. I visited friends and family in Albuquerque, my stepsister and her husband in San Francisco, and a friend in Moab, and I took a road trip to the Grand Canyon with my younger sister and her husband. I had time to swim laps with friends and attend a

Zumba class with a group of fun, great ladies. Better than working!

In late 2016, my aunt and I traveled to the beautiful Oregon coast in her camper van. I'd never done a road trip like that before, and it was fun! We visited many incredible national parks along the way. She's a great travel companion. The Oregon coast is one of her favorite places, and now I know why. Having enjoyable things to do with others helped a lot to offset the pain I felt when I was alone.

In early 2017, my aunt and I flew to Panama to visit my (other) younger brother and his sweet Panamanian wife. My stepsister and her husband joined us there. My brother moved to Panama seven years before our visit. It was impressive to watch him speak fluent Spanish. He's a phenomenal baker and chef, and they own a successful bakery and restaurant in Boquete. His nickname in the community is Senor Sugar, which we teased him about. One night, he was driving us home from the ocean when we were stopped at a routine checkpoint. It was nighttime, and police lights were flashing. He rolled down the window, and the cops recognized him and said, 'Hey, Senor Sugar'! We may have embarrassed him when everyone in the van started laughing! The trip was amazing! We went sightseeing, ziplining, and drove ATVs through the forest. We went through the Panama Canal, which was unbelievable! We all fell in love with beautiful, colorful Panama! My brother, stepsister, and I got to scatter our mom's ashes together on the shores of Panama. Nice! My husband's ashes are scattered there too. It was a very important time for me to be surrounded by my loving family and enjoy our time together.

Women showed up in my life from all over and were so caring and good for me - a great sisterhood. Women I knew casually invited me to paddle board or share other activities. A college friend just moved back here after her divorce, and we spent hours together just talking or enjoying many outdoor activities. I reconnected with a Nerd Herd friend, and we began regularly sharing our passion for hiking and photography. There's a saying which is – He who dies with the most toys wins! I have a saying which is "She who wears out the most pairs of hiking boots wins!" I was warmly welcomed into a peer group with my neighbors, who had been together for many years. One of my neighbors said that losing my husband gave them the gift of me. Those were heartfelt, profound words to hear and take into my heart. I'll say it again: women are amazing and awesome!

Men are great, too! One kind coworker kept asking me how he could help. Reluctantly, I finally said I needed one side of a fence built. He visited me, and we made a plan. He gathered nine engineers from his department, I knew them all, to come to my house and help me with all the outdoor projects we hadn't completed. This was before the life celebration. It was great! In a few hours, with so many guys helping, many projects were completed, including building the last side of the fence. They even brought a front loader to move gravel! They thought of other projects they could do for me while they were there. The weather was perfect, and there was laughter. I think we all enjoyed the day. I know I did! My job was to supervise. Beer and pizza were all they would take in return. My yard was in tip-top shape! This was a game changer for me and my dog. One of the nicest things to ever happen to me! I'm forever grateful.

I learned that it's okay to ask for help. Better than okay!

The first year without my husband was very hard to endure because it was the first time for everything—without him. All those special events and holidays where someone important was missing. The empty chair in a restaurant brought me to tears. We used to eat meals on the deck in nice weather. I couldn't bring myself to go out there to eat for a long time. I'd run into friends who didn't know, and I'd have to tell them. There were hundreds of firsts to get through. It started to get easier after getting through all those first times.

Trust that it will get easier.

The first Thanksgiving reminded me to be grateful for the many good things in my life. I wrote down this list and read it at Thanksgiving dinner with my family:

I'm thankful for my good health and being safe. My marriage to my husband. My loving family, here and in heaven. My dear friends, old, new, and in heaven. My sweet dog and good neighbors.

I'm thankful for a warm house, a comfy bed, and a hot shower. I'm thankful for all the clean water, food, clothing, healthcare, and clean air that I need.

I'm thankful I have land with a view, nice cars, money in the bank, cool toys, and beautiful jewelry.

I'm thankful for the good weather and to be living in Durango. I'm thankful for red wine, dark chocolate, hot coffee, cold beer, green chili, and Xanax.

I'm thankful for my hobbies, travels, music, and laughter. I'm thankful for my memories of the past, each new day, and what lies ahead.

***

The best thing I did for myself was bring Tai Chi Chih (TCC) back into my life. I learned how to do this moving meditation to help me deal with stress back in 1999 in Albuquerque. I didn't practice it regularly, but I never stopped practicing it completely. I knew I needed its power to heal. I attended an intensive training class in late 2017 in Albuquerque. I'd taught myself a few wrong ways to move over the years. I began practicing regularly and immediately felt the healing power.

I'm not someone who can sit in silence and meditate. I like moving meditations, such as gliding across a still lake in a kayak, with the cadence of the paddle stroking the water. Or the step-and-glide skiing down a trail in a forest in the winter while the snow falls gently. And Tai Chi Chih!

The focus of TCC is to activate, circulate, and balance the Chi (universal energy) inside of us. A practice consists of nineteen movements and takes thirty minutes to do. Because I was moving correctly again, my practices intensified the healing energy effect. I was finding balance again. Through this moving meditation, I found that place of peace, joy, and connection. Each time I went to that place, the experiences built on each other until it started becoming a more natural way to feel. I was becoming grounded, centered, and hopeful. Thoughts and feelings that trigger pain and fear lose their power when you're in a peaceful place.

The power of pain and fear faded as the power of peace and joy grew. Creating this power shift was key to helping heal my broken heart.

I decided to become a TCC teacher. I traveled to Albuquerque to work with a TCC teacher, and I reconnected with my first TCC teacher. They're great ladies! All the TCC practitioners I've met are great people. I completed the TCC teacher training and received my teacher certification in late 2018. Congratulations to me! TCC is very important in my life. The Chi is a great healer! There are countless stories of people healing from injuries, disease, and illness, and difficult mental struggles through practicing TCC. My dog loves TCC and joins me for my practice. I've taught many TCC classes, and I love it! I brought my dog to class whenever possible.

The Chi is also a great teacher! Occasionally, after my TCC practice, I will sit still and welcome the Chi in to teach me. My hands float to a comfortable position to the side, palms facing up. I feel warmth and peace. One day, my hands slowly moved toward each other, and then they stopped with palms facing each other. I could not push them together or pull them apart. I'd just made my first chi energy ball! I held the energy ball for a while, and then I sent it out into the world to do good. Now, I make energy balls often and easily. It's not something I can force. It happens without force. I know others who make energy balls, too!

Chi is there for everyone. It's in our cells.

I became interested in the Community Foundation in Durango, which is a nonprofit organization that supports other nonprofits throughout five counties. I met with the executive director in 2017 to learn more about it, and she invited me to join the finance committee, which I did. It was a great decision. The committee members were professionals from the community, and I enjoyed the robust discussions we had. I was learning and contributing. I was asked to join the board as the treasurer when the current treasurer moved away in 2020. It's refreshing and enjoyable to work with groups of people like this. Everyone is respectful and smart! They come from all types of backgrounds, and everyone brings something different to the group. It was a great way to engage my brain.

My aunt and I took another campervan road trip north to beautiful Banff, Canada, in late 2017. We both love photography, which adds a fun element to our trips. We play with our cameras, talk about photography, and swap tips. We had a great time. We went through Glacier NP on our way there, Yellowstone NP, and other beautiful places on our way back. I'm enjoying this way of traveling. In late 2019, we did a road trip around the Southwest. We visited many national parks, such as Antelope Canyon, Bryce, Zion, Grand Staircase, and Capital Reef. We got to know each other very well over the years. We're so lucky to have this time together! I look to her for guidance when I need it.

In late 2017, I met with a spiritual advisor for a reading. It wasn't to connect with my husband, and that's not what she's about. I just knew I needed to meet with her.

After our first reading, my mind was blown! She had many important messages that sent me down a path of discovery and awakening that changed my life. She did have one message from my husband. She said he wanted me to know he was with all the dogs. That made me so happy!

I met with my spiritual advisor once a year for three years. I'm so grateful she came into my life! My journey of discovery and awakening was important for my healing and for my life. This was my path to light and to my higher self. Did you know that light grows by passing it on? I've been on my path of self-discovery most of my life, especially in my thirties. This path took me to a whole other level! So many things I've always known or believed in were reinforced. I found answers to questions I'd always had. It's equally important to be open-minded and be discerning about what you do or don't resonate with. Not everything I discovered on my path was right for me. One of her most repeated and important messages to us all is this - Unity, Community, and Cooperation. That I believe in wholeheartedly! Remember those global issues I studied in college? Let me repeat that...

Unity, Community, and Co-operation!

Tragically, in mid-2018, both my stepmom and older sister died. My older sister died suddenly from a rare breast cancer. She chose not to fight it. She was fifty-eight, and she had five children. Her children chose to place her ashes with her husbands. My brother and I traveled with Dad to Santa Fe for her memorial service.

My dad and stepmom were married for over fifty years, and they were soul mates. My stepmom was very ill for the previous few years, and my dad took good care of her. She was holding on so tight to life! Once, when we were alone, I told her to talk to her angles, that she didn't have to suffer anymore, and that dad would be okay. Before long, she told me she'd talked to her angels, and she smiled. She died soon after that, on a sunny day in May. She was seventy-seven. She had her husband, son, and me there with her. Her death was very sad but also a blessing. Her life celebration was soon after, at my younger sister's house. I created a slideshow of her life with everyone's photos, which was enjoyed by all. Family and friends gathered to celebrate an amazing woman with a heart of gold. She's the best listener I've ever known, and she was always a best friend to me.

My mom's last husband remarried six months after she died. When he died, his current wife reached out to me in the fall of 2018. Our family got some of Mom's ashes, and he kept most of them. His wife wanted me to have them. It was about time! I'm grateful for this gesture. My aunt and I traveled to her house to get Mom's ashes and whatever else we wanted of Mom's remaining things. He kept a lot of her things and was very selective of what our family got. He kept her beautiful art, pottery, and jewelry. Unfortunately, he'd sold it all. I would've loved to buy some of it, especially my favorite pieces. Oh well, I can't change that now. I couldn't believe it when we found Mom's ashes in the cardboard box you get from the crematorium in a dusty warehouse! How could he do that!? That's just wrong! One of Mom's things I brought back is a beautiful pitcher from Mexico. It's handmade from pounded copper and is a work of art. I polished it, and that is now Mom's urn, which sits on the mantle over the fireplace. Much better! I'm certain Mom loves it.

Chapter Eight

Moving Forward

2019 to 2024

My dad, aunt, and I all share a unique bond that happens when you suffer the kind of loss we have. You can't truly understand it until it happens to you. Those of you who know, know. I didn't get it when mom lost her husband or when my aunt lost my uncle. I get it now. There's sympathy and empathy, which is very different from experiencing and knowing the pain of loss. When I meet other sweet souls who've suffered loss, we have that same bond. It's referred to as the club you never want to join. We often hug each other in that caring, knowing way. It helps a lot to know we are not alone.

Although I was active and doing better, I was still struggling a great deal because I go to bed alone and I wake up alone. Living alone is a completely different way of living than the life I'd always known. For the first time in my life, there's no one at home to talk to or share my da had absolutely no idea previously of how hard lo ness is. It's extremely hard! Thankfully, I'm enot completely alone. I have my super adorable dog to talk to and hug. He's a loving and happy dog. He's my daily companion and my joy. I needed the time I shared with my friends and family to help keep me sane. Loneliness is one of the hardest hurdles for me to overcome, if possible. I believe life is better shared, but if I can't share it, I can still live it!

Life is meant to be lived and meant to be cherished.

I took a big leap of faith in early 2019 when I signed up for a scuba diving trip to the Bahamas! I went with a local dive operation. I didn't know anyone, and I was nervous. I hadn't been scuba diving for five years. My husband and I logged one-hundred-twenty dives together over the years. I remember one morning, my husband and I were doing a lovely dawn dive from the shore in Bonaire. The scenic reef was teeming with life as the night turned into day. The octopuses were seeking shelter while the parrot fish were breaking free from the web they made to hold themselves to the coral. There was so much beauty, and my heart was overflowing with joy! I signaled to him that I could use a big hug! That's not easy with BC's, regulators, and air tanks on, so he reached around me and pinched my butt instead. We both took our regulators out of our mouths and smiled.

I keep saying that nothing nurtures like nature. Well, the ocean was missing from my life. I loved being back in the ocean again with all my favorite fish friends. I've missed them! The resort employees, dive crew, and divers were all great. The trip was not only a lot of fun, but it was also very healing. I'd learned to be brave again and to take risks. I'd come a very long way from the early days of grief when sometimes I wasn't brave enough to leave my house. The following year, I went to Belize with the same dive operation. I think I was a Belizean in a former life. I felt a connection there. It felt like home like I was with my brothers and sisters. It was a great trip, too!

I started to ride a mountain bike again. I'd made a new friend who helped me build and buy the perfect custom mountain bike for me. It's so fun to buy new toys! This sport helped me get back into the best physical shape I'd been in for many years. I wanted to ride the trails around Asheville, NC, where he lived. I checked that box with my new friend on my 60th birthday! We've had many fun adventures together since meeting in 2018. We connected instantly, and it felt like we'd known each other before.

I started to downhill ski again. I shared a locker at the local ski resort with my best friend for a couple of years. I bought all new ski gear that I love, which was fun! I skied with family and friends, but mostly with my best friend. We'd ski until lunchtime. Then we'd stop, get a beer for me and a bloody Mary for her, eat our sack lunches, and then ski some more. Those were great times. She moved away, and I don't ski at the resort as much anymore. I miss her!

So, my life coach was right after all! I survived, and I was thriving! I opened myself up to opportunities and my life was filling up again. Version 2.0 was doing good and moving forward. I'll say it again: everything we need is inside of us. That's not to say that we shouldn't lean on others for help and support. We should. I focused on myself, and I did the important internal work that needed to be done to help heal my broken heart.

Be open to whatever may come.
Seek the things that bring joy.
We must heal ourselves, as no one else can do it for us.

Through this internal work I've become what I call transparent. The things that used to hurt and trigger me pass through me now. One day, on a mountain bike trail, I came across the CEO who forced me out the door, and we spoke briefly. I realized I carry no anger towards her, which feels very good! I know and understand that she's on her journey, and I'm on mine. Figuratively and literally - the trail split, she went right, and I went left.

The one we hurt the most by our anger is ourselves.
I've learned to observe without judgment.

I was unemployed for three-and-a-half years. It was only going to be for one year originally. I did not want to go back to the same kind of high-level job I'd left, and I was undecided about what to do next. Luckily, the local golf course was looking for an accounting manager. Perfect! I like to play golf! It was a low-level job, which was a good fit. I got the job and started working in December 2019. I worked four days a week. I was paid half the salary I used to make, which was double what I needed to live on, plus free golf!

I have no debt, due to strategic financial planning.
This was essential to achieve my current lifestyle and minimal cash needs.

We had just opened the golf course when the COVID-19 Pandemic hit in April 2020. The world changed overnight. The year 2020 was an extremely hard year for everyone everywhere. Outdoor sports were a great escape. We had a place to escape! Gathering indoors was no longer an option, so our amazing team shut down the clubhouse, except for staff, and moved operations outside. I was grateful to have my job at the golf course. It not only gave me someplace to go to during such a difficult time, but it was also a positive environment. A win, win.

Almost everyone in my family got COVID, sometimes twice. I've managed to avoid the illness. Dad lost his taste and smell, which came back eventually, but not completely. Sadly, I know many people who have lost loved ones. My younger sister saw the worst of COVID as an MD during this time. She credited the team she worked with as giving her strength to help her cope. I started having dinner with Dad every Tuesday, a tradition that continues. We supported the local restaurants with take-out and spent hours talking and drinking wine at his dining room table. We got to know each other very well. He speaks honestly and has an interesting and wise perspective on everything! I appreciate his positive, optimistic outlook. Hmmm, I wonder if optimism is genetic. We make each other laugh. We continue to share stories about my husband and my stepmom often and about how lucky we are to have had them in our lives.

My dad played an important role in the Cold War with Russia, specifically with the nuclear disarmament treaties. He could not talk about work with us. After being retired for so long, he started to tell a few stories. Here's my favorite story of his. He was in Russia at an airplane hangar where four Russian bomber jets were on display. The pilot of each plane stood at attention in front of their plane. A tall, high-ranking Russian man stood next to Dad and didn't speak. Dad thought he might not know English. One of the planes was randomly chosen for inspection as part of the nuclear disarmament treaty. When the chosen plane was announced, the pilot had an uncharacteristic reaction when he smiled and pumped his fist. The Russian standing next to Dad leaned over and whispered in English - He just won the bet! Ha! My dad says Russians and Americans have more in common with each other than they have differences, and we all want the same things, such as avoiding a nuclear war.

We're all human, and I believe that most people are good.

I got the invitation of a lifetime in August 2020. I met this great guy at a fundraiser a year before. Much younger and happily married. He's a raft guide, and we talked about rafting in the Grand Canyon. I've always wanted to do that raft trip! We kept in touch, and one day, he invited me to go raft the Grand Canyon. Yes! This was a private trip with his college buddy and their friends. Rafts, supplies, staff, and transportation were provided by the commercial rafting company he worked for. He planned it with all his favorite hikes and campsites. It was his dream trip. It was for twelve days and covered 200 miles. The reason I got to go was because their friends in Sweden couldn't make it due to Covid. Unfortunate for them, but lucky for me! We all avoided getting COVID and showed up healthy.

I could not have dreamed of a better group of passengers and crew! I was warmly welcomed into the group. National parks had just started to re-open, and our group was one of the first to get a permit for the river. We practically had the whole place to ourselves! At the end of the trip, we took an exciting helicopter ride to a ranch on the canyon rim, where we enjoyed a shower and lunch. Then, a small plane flew us back to our parked cars at the launch site, and I drove home. It was one of the greatest trips of my life! Good people, fun times, and great memories! I'm forever grateful to my friend for including me!

The Grand Canyon is one of the most stunning places on Earth! The rock layer at the bottom is 1.7 billion years old! The Chi energy at river level down in the canyon is incredibly strong. It literally feeds the soul! I could get addicted to that feeling. I taught a few people some TCC movements, which was fun, and we did it throughout the trip. No one wanted to leave the canyon. We kept in touch afterward, and we shared with each other how very difficult it was to transition back into our lives after such a phenomenal trip in such a phenomenal place.

The rapids in the canyon were all exciting and fun. The hikes were all gorgeous. The campsites were all perfect. Many beautiful waterfalls feed the Colorado River. The miles of flat water allowed us time to soak in the surroundings. I had a special day when I scattered my husband's ashes on our wedding anniversary. The stand-out adventure for me was the hike to Thunder River, which shoots straight out of a canyon wall and is way up high! How unusual! The river flows down through the terrain, creating beautiful waterfalls. It was a very long, very hot hike, and I suffered in the heat. It was so worth it! Incredible! I also want to mention the astonishing turquoise-blue color of the Little Colorado River, where we spent hours one day. The conditions must be right to get that color, and we caught it at the perfect time. Nature is full of surprises!

Another Nerd Herd friend and I reconnected when her husband died a year after mine. She moved to Florida soon after he died. We stayed in touch, and then we traveled together to Juneau, Alaska, in June of 2021. We had great adventures whale watching, climbing glaciers, photographing bear cubs and eagles, sea kayaking, and much more. We traveled together again to Barcelona, Spain, in December 2021. This was my first trip to Europe. We fell in love with the beautiful, historic city of Barcelona as we explored the incredible sites and museums. We also had fun adventures in the surrounding areas of Barcelona. I wish people in America knew how to live life like the Spanish do. The relaxed pace of life and the sincere, kind attitude of the beautiful Spanish people are extraordinary! I could live there. It was a great place to bring in the new year!

The same good friend and I traveled to Maui, HI, in June of 2023. We had fun adventures, such as whale watching in a motorized raft, on a large sailboat, and kayaking. We enjoyed some beautiful hikes. We rented a convertible Mustang car for fun and to look cool! Tragically, Lahaina, Maui burned to the ground later that year. That was so devastating! We're glad we got to enjoy it before this terrible tragedy struck. We are both photographers, and sharing that passion is always fun for us when we travel. We have different styles, and I love her photography. We're great travel buddies and friends. *Fun Fact:* My friend was born in Russia and moved to America to marry her husband. She learned English in school as a child. Her English is excellent, and her Russian accent is lovely.

My stand-out adventure traveling with her involved a momma and baby humpback whales in Maui. Humpback whales come to the shallow waters of Maui to birth babies and breed. We were out with a guided group in clear bottom kayaks, hoping to see whales. On a serene, still morning, we paddled a long way out to a lovely place to snorkel. We enjoyed snorkeling for a while. Then we got back in our kayaks to have a beverage and snack. We were enjoying our snacks when suddenly a huge momma humpback whale floated to the surface about fifty feet away! Then her baby appeared! We all became very quiet and very still. There were continuous mild swells coming through. We rose up and down with the swells in our kayaks, and so did the whales. Momma was resting, breathing, and blowing mist into the air. It was one of the most wonderful and tranquil sounds I've ever heard! There's no food source for the whales in those waters, so I imagine resting is vital for these mommas and probably hard to come by with all the males wanting to breed. The baby was exercising and learning how to use her body. She rolled around, showing us her fins and tail. This went on for quite a while. It was hard to resist the urge to jump in and watch them from below! Momma decided to either join the fun, or show her baby how it's done, I'm not sure which. Momma rolled over and showed us her huge fin. Wow! Then they disappeared under the water's surface and were gone. I could've stayed there all day riding the swells together and listening to the momma breathe. This encounter was so intimate and joyful, and something I'm incredibly grateful for.

There's a saying I like, which is - There are friends for a reason, friends for a season, and friends for life. One of the greatest things in life is all the different people who pass through our spheres as we travel on our journeys. I think almost all friends are friends for a reason. Some more than others.

A good example of friends for a season was the group of lady coworkers that became good friends. For a few years, we enjoyed gathering at each other's homes to drink margaritas and eat appetizers. Occasionally, we gathered at a bar. There were some very funny ladies among us, and sometimes things got a little crazy! We laughed a lot and just had fun! The company where we all worked was merged with another, and many of us were laid off, so we went our separate ways. It sure was fun while it lasted!

A good example of friends for life is a best friend I had when we were fourteen. We went our separate ways after high school. Many decades later, I opened a Facebook account, and she found me! She lives in Sweden, where she spent her adult life. We kept in touch, and we finally got to see each other again after more than forty years when she visited her aunt in Albuquerque in 2024. That was fun! Reconnecting with her has been great! *Fun Fact:* My friend is the Executive Director of a nonprofit organization that addresses environmental issues globally. She's a self-proclaimed fierce warrior for Mother Earth!

Friendships, like life, continually change. For example, a single friend got married, and a married friend got divorced. I started spending more time with the single one and less time with the married one, which makes sense since I'm single. I traveled with the newly single friend to Sedona, AZ, and then again to Zion National Park in Utah. We had a great time hiking in these two spectacular places. She's a fun travel companion, a good friend, and a regular hiking and paddle-boarding buddy.

My stand-out adventure traveling with her was the popular hike to Angels Landing in Zion. It was crowded and somewhat treacherous. There's a pole and chain system to hold on to if needed. The view at the landing was a great reward for the effort. It was jaw-dropping and expansive! While at the top, a very rare giant condor bird with a seven-foot wingspan flew by right in front of us! What a unique experience that was! There are nine condors residing in Zion. We had the great fortune of seeing seven of them.

This is another example of why I've lived my life outside.
It's the special experiences that only happen when you go outside!

The year 2022 was going along fine until one day in September. On that day, I'd done a high altitude eight-mile hike followed by a round of golf. While driving home, my back and right leg seized up with terrible pain. I had to pull off the road until the pain passed. The next morning, I woke up to terrible pain. I had a herniated disk in my lower back! It was debilitating! I had excruciating nerve pain that shot from my back, through my right hip, and down my right leg to my ankle. There are no words to describe the pain. Sitting down was the worst thing I could do. I spent most of my waking hours standing up. I took strong painkillers at night to try to get some sleep. Getting out of bed and being in a car was torture! Fortunately, I could work remotely from home, and I traveled to the office for an hour or two once or twice a week. Walking was my relief and my way to heal, and I walked three times a day. At first, I could only walk with walking sticks to the end of my long driveway, and it was two months before I could drive again.

During this time, my (other) brother visited from Panama with his wife and daughter. The visit had been planned before I was injured. My aunt visited, too. My family in Durango joined us at my house for a potluck party. Both of my younger brothers are great cooks. The one that lives here brought smoked meat, which is his specialty. My sister brought her specialty, a delightful, healthy salad. My specialty is wine. I was able to get around well enough, and we all had a great time. We called it the Party-of-the-Year! We were graced with the Sunset-of-the-Year that day, too! My Panamanian sister-in-law loves my dog a lot. I'd taught him some Spanish to impress her. She thought that was great!

Facing this endurance test while living on my own was hard! Not only is life better shared, but it's also much easier. There were times when I needed something in another room, and I just wanted someone else to go get it for me, to make dinner, to feed the dog, and to help me with all the small things. The pain made doing small things hard, and I was exhausted! Thank goodness I had family and friends who helped me with driving and shopping. All you can do with an injury like mine is give it time to heal. I also did physical therapy, and I worked with the same gifted personal trainer that my husband worked with. She shared stories about my husband, which I enjoyed a lot. She said the group of women he worked out with did their best to embarrass him, but it didn't work, and that they all adored him. I knew he enjoyed working out with those women, and he thought they were crazier and more explicit than men are when they get together. My right leg was weak and thin, and it had a lot of catching up to do with my left leg. I focused on getting stronger, and I was doing much better by December.

The following May, my friend who lives in Asheville invited me to go backpacking for three days on the Appalachian Trail in Virginia with his friends. I went with them, and I carried over thirty pounds on my back! We had fun, and I felt great! I prepared for the trip by adding a canvas bag filled with twenty pounds of rocks to my daypack for day hikes. It looked funny, but it did the trick!

In late 2023, I left my job at the golf course and went to work for the Community Foundation (CF) as the Finance Director. The CF lost its Finance Director suddenly and needed someone. After serving on the finance committee and the board, the opportunity with the CF seemed like a good fit, and I knew I could help. It was hard to leave the golf course and my friends there. That was a fun job with fun and good people, both the staff and the golfers. I miss them!

I could've retired by this time. However, retiring didn't interest me because I'm single, and that made retirement seem less enjoyable to me. I'd become accustomed to the loneliness and okay with the single life, but I hadn't embraced it yet. I considered working my escape from being alone. I planned to be at the CF for three years, maybe more.

Surprisingly, within six months, something significant shifted inside my heart. Suddenly, more than anything, I wanted to retire! I gave the CF four months' notice. I'm grateful for the opportunity to work with the staff, non-profits, philanthropists, board and committee members. I have great respect for all of them and for what they do for the community. I had no idea previously just how much help is needed, provided, and funded. It's remarkable! It was a great career. When it's time, it's time!

**There's still so much to see and do!
And I'm still young at heart.**

The rest of my story is yet to be written. I'm calling myself version 3.0. I'm open to whatever comes my way. I've learned that the heart always has room for more. Life is to be cherished and I will seek out joy and beauty.

It's been eight years since my husband died, and I still think about him often. So many things trigger memories, and my memories are happy ones, even when I wipe the occasional tear from my eyes. I miss him with gratitude for the thirty-two years he gave me, from my twenties to my fifties.

I lived with him by my side for over half of my life.
I am who I am because of our union.
He is, and always will be, a part of me.
The best part of me.

When it's my time to die, I won't be surprised if my husband comes to get me on the wings of a raven....

Made in the USA
Coppell, TX
15 February 2025

45951864R00083